LONDON

A THOUSAND AND ONE

INTRIGUING FACTS

LONDON

A THOUSAND AND ONE
INTRIGUING FACTS

Compiled by

GILL DAVIES

◆ BOOK ◆ BLOCKS ◆

This edition first published 2004 by Book Blocks
an imprint of CRW Publishing Limited
69 Gloucester Crescent, London NW1 7EG

ISBN 1 904 633 91 9

Text © CRW Publishing Limited 2004

1 3 5 7 9 10 8 6 4 2

Some of the data in this book has been extracted from
London! London! London!
a timeline history

Compiled by Gill Davies
Typeset in Great Britain by Playne Books Limited
Printed and bound in China by Imago

CONTENTS

Big Ben

WESTMINSTER

WESTMINSTER
8

1

1721–42

Britain's first Prime Minister was
Robert Walpole.

2

1783

The youngest ever Prime Minister was
William Pitt the Younger,
aged 24.

3

William Gladstone was Prime Minister four times:
1868–74, 1880–85, 1886 and 1892–94.

4

Completed in 1680, Downing Street was named after the
man who built it. Usually
the Prime Minister lives at number 10
the Chancellor of the Exchequer lives at number 11
The Chief Whip lives at number 12.

5

1979–90
Margaret Thatcher was Britain's (and Europe's) first woman
Prime Minister.

6

The word parliament is derived from the French *parler*
meaning 'to talk'.

1530s

Henry VIII established his court at Whitehall Palace. Since then Whitehall has been the site of principal government offices.

A suffragette handcuffed herself to a statue in St Stephen's Hall. You can still see where the statue's sword had to be cut in order to remove her!

The House of Commons mace
is a symbol of Royal authority.
It is set on the table in front of the Speaker.
Without it, the House cannot sit and debate.

10

The House of Lords has been a distinct element of Parliament since the 1200s.

11

1500s
Whitehall was the largest palace in Europe.

12

The Lord Chancellor sits on the Woolsack. The tradition dates back to the reign of Edward III when the wool trade was a most important part of the economy.

13

The Parliament buildings have over 1,000 apartments and cover more than 8 acres (3.24 hectares).

14

Black Rod, a personal attendant of the sovereign,
is named after his staff of office –
an ebony stick surmounted with a golden lion.

15

At the State Opening of Parliament,
the door is slammed in Black Rod's face.
He has to knock three times before he is admitted!
This symbolises the right of the Commons to debate
without interference.

16

The Great Seal is a large silver seal used to stamp official
documents from the Sovereign. A new seal has been made
for each monarch since William the Conqueror.

17

Before the State Opening of Parliament, the Yeoman Warders search the cellars of the Houses of Parliament to ensure there is no repeat of the Gunpowder Plot, when Guy Fawkes attempted to blow up the building.

18

The name Great Scotland Yard derives from the apartments in Whitehall reserved for visiting kings of Scotland (prior to Union with Scotland in 1603).

19

The most famous Lord Mayor of London was Dick Whittington, who served three times in 1397–99, 1406–7 and 1419–20. A mercer, he supplied fine fabrics to the royal court and lent money to the king.

1485

The Yeoman of the Guard were founded by Henry VII. They wear a distinctive red uniform dating back to Tudor times and are often called Beefeaters.

1097

Westminster Hall was built under the direction of William Rufus (son of William the Conqueror) and is the largest Norman hall in Europe.

Westminster Hall hosted the trials of Charles I, Guy Fawkes and Sir Thomas More, the abdication of Edward II and the deposition of Richard II.

23

1649

Charles I was executed outside the Banqueting House, Whitehall Palace.

24

Big Ben is actually the name of the bell in the clock tower of the Houses of Parliament.

25

1834

When someone decided to burn the Exchequer's medieval wooden tally rods in a chamber below the House of Lords, the Houses of Parliament burned down. The new Palace of Westminster was built in its place.

Rodin's *The Burgers of Calais* depicts the brave men who were hostages to England's King Edward III in 1347 during the 100 Years War.

Big Ben bell was named after either Sir Benjamin Hall, Chief Commissioner of Works for Westminster, or (less likely) boxer and local pub landlord Benjamin Caunt of St Martin's Lane.

Each of the clock's four dials has a diameter of 23ft (7.01m), the minute hands are 14ft (4.27m) long and the numerals on each face are nearly 2ft (61cm) high.

29

Big Ben weighs 13.5 ton (13,760kg). When it was cast it was Britain's heaviest bell.

30

Big Ben bell is 9ft (2.74m) diameter and 7ft 6ins (2.29m) high.

31

The accuracy of the clock's time is controlled by placing old pennies in the mechanism.

32

A light at the top of St Stephen's tower indicates that the House of Commons is sitting.

33

Big Ben was cast on 10 April 1858:
the first chime rang in Westminster on 31 May 1859.

34

The two most popular London attractions for overseas
visitors are St Paul's Cathedral and Big Ben.

35

Boswell (Scottish man of letters)
claimed to have made love on Westminster Bridge.

36

William Caxton rented premises in
Westminster Abbey precincts and then set up England's
first printing press in a shop by the Chapter House.

37

AD **785**

Monks were living and working here.
Westminster Abbey stands on the grounds
of a former Benedictine monastery.

38

1065

Edward the Confessor built a new church
on the site of the Benedictine monastery.

39

Many kings and queens are buried near the shrine of
Edward the Confessor or in Henry VII's Chapel.

1245

Henry III pulled down the church and replaced it with the
Abbey but he saved the nave.

1066

William the Conqueror was crowned in Westminster. Since
then almost every coronation has
been held in Westminster Abbey (except for Edward V
and Edward VIII).

Memorials in Westminster Abbey include one to the first
man in London to carry an umbrella.

1760

The last monarch buried in the abbey was George II.
(Since then, sovereigns have been buried at
Windsor Castle.)

1400

Chaucer was buried in Westminster Abbey. Since then,
Poet's Corner has been the resting place of many authors,
including Browning, Dr Johnson, Wordsworth, Dickens,
Hardy, Milton, Kipling and Tennyson.

Ben Jonson, requesting economy of space, was buried
vertically in Poet's Corner.

1989

The last person to be buried in Poet's Corner was actor
Laurence Olivier.

Poet's Corner has now been declared full!

The Grave of the Unknown Warrior in Westminster Abbey
holds the remains of a World War I soldier brought back
from Flanders after the war.

Sir Walter Raleigh is buried at
St Margaret's, Westminster.

50

Henry V
(with his Agincourt helmet, shield and saddle)
is buried in Westminster Abbey.

51

Roman Catholic Westminster Cathedral was built by the
Victorians using more than 12 million bricks.

52

Westminster Cathedral's nave is the widest in the country.

53

Westminster Cathedral's campanile is over
270 feet (82.30m) high.

54

Samuel Pepys (1655)
and Winston Churchill (1908)
were both married at St Margaret's Westminster.

55

Every Christmas,
Norway sends a huge Christmas tree
to stand in Trafalgar Square,
as a thank-you for Britain's help during World War II.

56

Winston Churchill's
underground Cabinet War Rooms
are below King Charles Street.

Nelson's Column in Trafalgar Square is 183ft 9ins (56m)
high; the figure of Nelson measures 16ft 5ins (5m) and
stands on a 167ft 4ins (51m) column.
The four lions arrived in 1868.

Nelson's Column was built to commemorate
Admiral Nelson's victory against Napoleon at Trafalgar
in Spain in 1805.

Westminster Bridge

WESTMINSTER

St James's Palace, Pall Mall

WEST END

Temple Bar from the Strand

59

Leicester Square was named after the Earl of Leicester who developed the area in the early 1600s.

60

Covent Garden was London's first square, originally developed it in the 1630s by Inigo Jones.

61

In the mid–1700s Covent Garden had many brothels masquerading as Turkish baths.

62

Mayfair is named after a notorious, bawdy fair – banned in the early 1700s because of its 'drunkenness, fornication, gaming and lewdness'!

Haymarket was named after a foul-smelling hay market
that existed on the site until 1830.

Haymarket was popular with prostitutes until the early
1900s as many wealthy men visited the theatres there.

The name Pall Mall came from a game like croquet called
pallo a maglio, popular with Charles II and played
regularly in Pall Mall and The Mall.

The London Library is the oldest private library in Britain,
founded 1841.

In 1807, Pall Mall was London's first gas-lit street.

1833

The Duke of York's Column by St James's Park
was paid for by stopping soldiers' wages for a day!

Piccadilly Circus was named after the picadils (high ruffed
collars) made by a local tailor and collar maker.

Beautiful colonnades at the Regent Street Quadrant were
torn down in 1848 after complaints that they encouraged
prostitution.

71

In the 1770s Portland Place was the widest street
in London.

72

Bond Street is named after Sir Thomas Bond who, with
others, purchased the land in the late 1600s.

73

The Beatles gave their last performance on the roof of their
offices in Savile Row in 1969.

74

Five of the Cato Street Conspirators, who planned to
murder the Cabinet in 1820, were the last men in
Britain to be beheaded.

P. G. Wodehouse's fictional Jeeves & Wooster lived in Half Moon Street, close to Piccadilly.

Oxford Street was so called because it was originally the main Roman route to Oxford.

In the 1700s, Oxford Street was known as Tyburn Road because it was part of the route prisoners took to the Tyburn Gallows at Marble Arch.

During the 1700s, Oxford Street was the site of circuses and tiger baiting.

79

The name Soho derives from the hunting call of 'Soe Hoe!'

80

Soho, infamous in the 1970s for its strip clubs, is now one
of Europe's leading gay centres.

81

Mr Gerrard, Sir Francis Compton and Mr Frith
developed the area in the late 1600s;
each has a street in Soho named after him.

82

1819

Burlington Arcade, Piccadilly, was built by Lord Cavendish
to stop rubbish being thrown into his garden.

Chinatown (near Leicester Square) is a centre for London's 60,000-strong Chinese community but few of them actually live there.

At the crossroads of Berwick and Broadwick Streets is a replica of a water pump that caused the deaths of over 500 Soho residents in the cholera epidemic of 1854.

At Apsley House, a portrait by Goya of Wellington began as a painting of Joseph Bonaparte. Goya superimposed Wellington's head after Bonaparte's defeat.

Cheapside, Poultry and Bucklersbury

CITY
OF LONDON

86

Around 5,000 people live in the City of London.

87

Over 300,000 commute into the City of London
each day to work.

88

There have been more than 670 Lord Mayors of London.

89

1189

The first recorded Mayor of London was
Henry FitzAilwyn.

1216

saw the first Lord Mayor's show or pageant.

Since 1752 Lord Mayors of London have lived in Mansion House, opposite the Bank of England.

Mansion House has several staterooms – and a cell once occupied by suffragette Emmeline Pankhurst.

1199

King John granted the citizens of the City of London the right to elect their own sheriffs.

94

Dick Whittington, the fairy-tale character, is based on
Richard Whittingron who was Lord Mayor of London
three times – in the 1420s – and did marry
Alice FitzWarin.

95

1215

The citizens' right to elect a mayor annually was granted
by King John in a charter.

96

London's share of foreign-exchange trading
is more than that of
New York and Tokyo combined.

1384

The wards of the City elected the first
Common Council.

London holds some 20% of the global total for cross-border
international bank lending.

The London foreign-exchange market is the largest
in the world – 32% of global turnover.

The Bank of England was founded in 1694 and has
issued banknotes ever since.

101

One billion banknotes are made each year by the
Bank of England.

102

There are more foreign banks in London (over 570)
than anywhere else in the world.

103

Foreign banks manage over 50% of UK banking-sector
assets, some £2,600 billion.

104

Author of *The Wind in the Willows*, Kenneth Grahame, was
a secretary at the Bank of England.

105

Bank emblems include:

an eagle (Barclays)

a grasshopper (Martins)

a cat and fiddle (Commercial Bank of Scotland)

an artichoke (Alexanders).

106

One Lord Mayor built a bridge over Seething Lane
to connect his two houses – without permission.
His fine of a freshly plucked rose
is still presented by his descendants
each year to the Lord Mayor.

1836

A sewer worker discovered a tunnel into the Bank of England's bullion vaults. He arranged to meet the directors there and emerged from below a flagstone. He was rewarded; the tunnel was blocked in!

Sir Francis Child, Lord Mayor in 1698, is credited with having founded the banking profession.

1680s

Lloyd's insurance was launched, providing marine insurance to ship captains and merchants.

110

1909

Lloyd's of London first motor policy issued.

111

1911

Lloyd's of London first aviation policy.

112

The term 'underwriters' originated when those sharing the
risk signed their names one below the other on the policy.

113

In 1760, 150 Lloyd's brokers formed a club
to buy and sell shares.

Lloyd's has underwritten policies insuring:

114

the nose of a whisky distiller.

115

against crocodile attack in Australia.

116

food critic Egon Ronay's taste buds (£250,000).

117

against the fatal bites of poisonous spiders found under lavatory seats in Australia.

118

Betty Grable's 'million dollar legs'.

119

a 2000-year-old wine jar and contents.

120

an elephant and a unicorn for Barnum
and Bailey circus promoters.

121

the world's largest cigar –
length 12ft 6ins (3.81m), weight 242lb (110k) –
for its retail value of £17,933.35.

122

a sea-going bathtub –
provided the plug stayed in place at all times!

Lloyd's has underwritten policies insuring:

123

against the possibility of Kerry Wallace's hair failing to
grow back again after being shaved off for
a *Startrek* film.

124

Gene Kelly

Mae West

Elizabeth Taylor

Frank Sinatra

Edward G. Robinson

Bob Hope

Bing Crosby

Richard Burton and Sir Laurence Olivier.

125

1773

Lloyd's members called themselves the
Stock Exchange.

126

The Baltic Exchange is the world's largest self–regulated
ship-broking market.

127

Almost 30% of the UK's financial-services employment is
in the City – 8.4% of total jobs in London.

128

Smithfield was the site of horse fairs, jousting tournaments
and public executions.

129

St Bartholomew's Fair in Smithfield was held annually to raise money for St Bartholomew's Hospital.

130

Blackfriars is named after a Dominican monastery that stood there until the 15th century.

131

1500s

Shakespeare had a house in Blackfriars.

132

1123

St Bartholomew's Hospital was founded.

1537

St Bartholomew's Hospital was dissolved by Henry VIII.

1544

St Bartholomew's Hospital was rescued.

135

The ancient city wall had seven gates: Aldgate, Bishopsgate, Moorgate, Cripplegate, Aldersgate, Newgate and Ludgate.

Bunhill Fields has been a plague pit and a burial ground for Dissenters. William Blake and John Bunyan are buried here.

1666

Four fifths of the City burnt down in the Great Fire.

100,000 Londoners died in the Great Plague, which struck
London in 1664–65.

The 'freedom of the City' is granted by the Corporation of
London. Recipients include Nelson Mandela, Florence
Nightingale and Winston Churchill.

AD 979

King Ethelred levied the earliest customs duty.

141

1382

The first Custom House was built,
close to the present building.

142

1500

The first printing press was set up in Fleet Street.

143

National Westminster Tower (52 storeys and 600 feet high)
was once the tallest building in Europe.

144

The Corporation of London is the oldest local authority
in England.

Accused of stealing sandwiches,
a builder in Philpot Lane was pushed to his death.
The real culprits were mice,
now commemorated by a carving.

1755

Publication of England's first comprehensive dictionary,
compiled by Dr Samuel Johnson,
who lived in Gough Square.

The road of London Wall follows the line of the old Roman
wall, parts of which can still be seen.

148

John Wesley, founder of Methodism,
lived at 47 City Road until 1791.
Next door is the chapel where
PM Margaret Thatcher was married.

149

The 202ft (61.57m) Monument marks the start of the
Great Fire in Pudding Lane in 1666.

150

The Monument is the world's tallest free-standing
stone column.

151

The Monument has 311 steps.

The Old Bailey, site of many famous trials, is built where Newgate Prison stood.

1411

The Guildhall was built for the medieval trade guilds.

Built 1844

The Royal Exchange was the first financial trading marketplace in London.

St Paul's Whispering Gallery is reached via 259 steps.

St Paul's Cathedral was built after the Great Fire of London
and was completed in 1710.

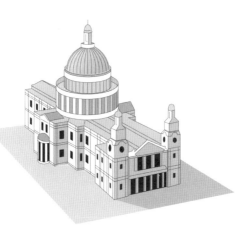

Grapes Inn, Limehouse

EAST END

Petticoat Lane (Middlesex Street), 1870

157

The East End area still has seven working farms.

158

Londoners who live in the East End are called 'cockneys' – from the Middle English 'cokeney' meaning 'cock's egg' or 'misshapen egg'.

159

It is said that a true cockney must be born within the sound of 'Bow Bells' (the bells of Bow Church).

160

Brick Lane was built on the site where many brick kilns worked to help rebuild the city after the Great Fire in 1666.

161

Once many costermongers sold fruit or vegetables
from barrows in the street.

162

Traders dealing with goods of dubious origin were referred
to as 'duffers'.

163

1600s
The first immigrants were French Protestant Huguenots
who set up silk-weaving businesses in Spitalfields.

164

By 1700, there were 10,000 houses in the parish
of Stepney.

165

Between 1560 and 1640 only 14% of Stepney inhabitants were native-born Londoners.

166

Britain's most infamous serial killer, Jack the Ripper, killed at least five victims in Whitechapel in 1888.

167

Captain Cook met his wife in an East End inn when she was only a sickly child, daughter of the landlord.
He married her in 1762.

168

Bells have been made at Whitechapel for 500 years.

169

The bells for Westminster Abbey were made at the Whitechapel bell foundry.

170

Aldgate was named after one of the seven gates that led into the ancient City of London.

171

1900

Many Jews immigrated to the East End. In some streets over 90% of the inhabitants were Jewish.

172

Dickens's Pickwickians set off for Ipswich from the *Bull Inn*, which was situated just off Aldgate High Street.

Westminster's Big Ben was recast at Whitechapel when the original bell cracked.

Joseph Merrick (the 'Elephant Man') was discovered in a freak show on the Mile End Road.

In 1907, a meeting in a Hackney chapel of the Russian Social Democratic Labour Party was allegedly attended by Lenin, Stalin, Trotsky, Gorky and Litvinov.

1788 – 1960
London was the biggest port in the world.

177

In 1930, 100,000 men employed in the London docks handled 35 million tons of cargo.

178

Wapping, colonised since Anglo Saxon times, got its name from a tribesman called Waeppa.

179

Limehouse got its name from limeoasts – kilns where chalk was burnt to make lime for London buildings.

180

Some claim that the Isle of Dogs was so-called because it was the site for Henry VIII's kennels.

(*see* 743 Ghosts)

181

Canary Wharf's 800ft (243.84m) tower, One Canada Square, has 50 storeys and 1,200,00 square feet (111,480 sq m) of office space. It is one of the tallest buildings in Europe.

182

Charles I's executioner, who lived in Whitechapel, obtained an orange stuffed with cloves from the king's pocket and sold this for ten shillings.

183

760 skeletons have been uncovered in excavations by Tower Bridge. Black Death corpses were slung into plague pits here in 1348 and 1350.

184

We know Shakespeare lived for a time at Bishop's Gate, Shoreditch, because he was noted in records as a tax defaulter!

185

The new *Globe Theatre* is set just 200 yards from Shakespeare's original playhouse.

186

Over 300 people were put to death on Tower Hill.

187

A number of pirates were hung at Execution Dock, Wapping – including Captain Kydd in 1701.

Wapping was home to:

188

explorer Captain Cook.

189

Zachariah Hicks, who first sighted Australia.

190

Captain Bligh of *Mutiny on the Bounty* fame.

191

The Tower of London has been a palace, prison and castle,
as well as home to the Crown Jewels and
a famous place of execution.

Cockney rhyming slang includes the following:

alligator – later

apples and pears – stairs

bricks and mortar – daughter

Bristol City – titty

cash and carried – married

coals and coke – broke

currant bun – sun

daft and barmy – army

daisy roots – boots

ding dong – song

Donald Duck – luck

elephant's trunk – drunk

Jack Tar – bar

Joanna – piano

mother's ruin – gin

Mozart and Liszt – pissed (drunk)

needle and pin – gin

Noah's Ark – park

Oedipus Rex – sex

plates of meat – feet

tiddly wink – drink

trouble and strife – wife

trunks of trees – knees

Queen Elizabeth I

A BRIEF HISTORY

London Docks

A BRIEF HISTORY

5000-3000 BC

Tools from this time found in Hackney Brook.

1008 BC

Legend has it that London was founded now. Prehistoric remains and inscribed coins have established existence of a pre-Roman city.

620 BC

King Lud built walls and towers around his city; his name lives on in Ludgate, and London, for the name derived from Lud's-town.

196

To the north lay a great moor and fen that survive in the names Moorfields and Finsbury.

197

The town was bounded by the River Fleet and marshes. The Thames flowed through low-lying land, often flooding and creating one vast lake.

198

The western island (now crowned by St Paul's Cathedral) was the site of a British settlement which existed before the coming of the Romans.

Islets had place-names ending in 'ey' or 'ea', such as
Bermondsey, Thorney, Battersea and Chelsea.

Trading boats arrived via the Thames and London became a
place of primitive commerce.

55 BC

Julius Caesar invaded England.

AD 42–43

The Romans arrived. The capital of the Roman occupation
was established at 'Londinium', later restored and fought over.

AD 43–60

The Roman settlement built a walled enclosure of 330
acres (133.55 hectars) and the town grew in size to become
a busy mercantile centre.

AD 61

The *Annals of Tacitus* described 'Londinium' as 'not
dignified with the name of a colony but celebrated for the
gathering of dealers and commodities'.

AD 61

The Roman city (called Augusta then) was captured by
Boadicea whose rebel troops massacred the inhabitants.

AD 312–14

During the latter part of the Roman occupation the city was Christianised.

All the churches in Thames Street,
the oldest part of the city, were dedicated to
the Apostles and not to later saints,
so it is likely that they occupied the sites
of early Christian churches.

AD 314

Restitutus, Bishop of London, was present at the Council of Arles.

400s

When the Saxons drove out the Romans and the Britons,
London was one of the few places to survive continuously.

400s

Final withdrawal of the Roman legions. Celts, Saxons and
Danes battled for supremacy.

AD 604

St Mellitus was sent by St Augustine
to be the first Bishop of London.
The line of bishops lasted nearly a thousand years.

AD 839

London sacked by Danes.

AD 871–99

Under Alfred the Great, Londoners defeated the
Danes and enjoyed peace and prosperity.

AD 886

London became an important town under
King Alfred, who rebuilt the city defences
and created a government.

215

AD 895

London attacked by Danes.

216

900s

London Bridge built, the only bridge to span the Thames.

217

AD 924–39

At the time of Athelstan
(Alfred's grandson),
London needed eight 'moneyers'
to produce coinage.

1000s

The Danes harassed London and the city was caught up in
the struggle between Canute and Edmund Ironside.

1013–14 & 1017–35

During Canute's reign, 14% of his revenue came from
London.

1042–66

Edward the Confessor resided chiefly at Westminster,
where he rebuilt Westminster Abbey in which his
relics are still enshrined.

221

1066

Norman invasion. William the Conqueror defeated King
Harold at Hastings and was crowned king in
Westminster Abbey.

222

1066

William the Conqueror established a strong rule and had
the White Tower (the keep of the Tower of London) built
just east of the city wall.

223

1066–1180

Under the Normans and Plantagenets, the city grew
commercially and politically.

1087

London consisted of low wooden houses
thatched with reeds or straw.
In this year, one of the frequent fires burned
the greater part of the city.

1087

St Paul's was rebuilt:
the new cathedral
was one of the largest churches in
Europe at 600 feet (183 metres) long.

1189–99

During the reign of Richard I,
a form of municipal government was set up,
from which the modern
City Corporation developed.

1091

A new London Bridge replaced one washed
away by great floods.

1100

Citizens gained a new charter from Henry I – confirmed by
Stephen in 1135.

1118

The Knights Templar established themselves
in Holborn,
moving to Fleet Street later,
where the Temple Church
(consecrated 1185) remains.

1136

Another great fire destroyed the city
from Ludgate to St Paul's.

1135–54

King Stephen's rule.
Civil War raged between Stephen and Matilda.
When Matilda deprived London of its charters, the
citizens drove her from the city. London rose to
the position of a capital.

1176

Peter of Colechurch, a priest, began the
rebuilding of London Bridge with stone.
It took 33 years to build but lasted for 700 years.

1189

Court of aldermen decreed that houses must be built of
stone instead of wood to check the disastrous fires, but
wooden houses continued to spring up.

1189–1212

Henry Fitz-alwyne became the first
Mayor of London under the title of 'bailiff'.

1215

King John granted the city the right to elect a
mayor annually.

1221

The Dominicans established themselves in Holborn –
and in Blackfriars by 1276

1240–1315

A new Gothic choir and a
tower built in St Paul's.

1245

Westminster Abbey rebuilt by Henry III and
finished in 1295.

239

1250

St Saviour's, Southwark, built.

240

1285

Edward I deprived citizens of their right
to elect a Lord Mayor –
not regained until 1297.

241

1290

Jews (who since the 11th century had lived in
Old Jewry) expelled from England.

1200s-1400s

During the Middle Ages, guilds gained control of civic affairs.

1300s

Each trade had its own locality as the street

names suggest:

Milk Street

Bread Street

Wood Street

Fish Street

Poultry Street

Friday Street . . .

was the market for Friday's dried fish.

The city now had 13 large churches and 126 parish churches.

1349

A great plague killed half the population of England.

1371

Charterhouse built near where plague victims were buried.

1381

Wat Tyler's rebellion.

1397–1419

Lord Mayor of London, Sir Richard Whittington
built Newgate, Christ's Hospital,
much of St Bartholomew's Hospital
and the chapel and
library at the Guildhall.

1400

Death of Geoffrey Chaucer at Westminster.

1407

Plague checked the growth of the population.

1411

Guildhall rebuilt; during the century the walls and gates
were strengthened.

1473

Caxton set up the first English printing press at
Westminster – soon followed by Wynkyn de Worde,
Pynson, and other great printers.

1483

Murder of Edward V and his brother,
the Princes in the Tower.

1506, 1517, 1528 & 1551

Outbreaks of 'sweating sickness' killed thousands.

1500

30,000 Londoners died of the plague.

Nevertheless the city continued to prosper.

1502–17

Henry VII's fine Perpendicular chapel was added to
Westminster Abbey.

1512

Royal palace at Westminster burned.

1529

Henry VIII took possession of Wolsey's palace,
York Place, and renamed it Whitehall.

1530

Henry VIII began to build St James's Palace.

1534

Henry VIII obtained an Act of Parliament abolishing papal authority.

1535

The Act of Supremacy made Henry VIII Supreme Head of the Church in England.

1535–36

Many martyrs, including Sir Thomas More, died. Religious houses and the monasteries fell.

1543–1550

Anthony van den Wyngaerde produced his panorama.

1547

Substitution of English for Latin in all churches.
Property belonging to colleges and chantries was
seized for royal use, and the great city guilds had
to redeem their lands at a cost of £20,000.

1558

Accession of Elizabeth I.

1570

Martyrdoms resumed and reached a peak in 1588. London became a Protestant city.

1588

Spanish Armada.

1570–1600

An undated map is attributed to Agas.

1572

The first actual dated map, by Hoefnagel.

270

1566

Royal Exchange founded by Sir Thomas Gresham.

271

1558–1603

Elizabeth I's reign brought great wealth, power and overseas trading to London.

272

1599

Shakespeare's *Globe Theatre* built.

273

Late 1500s

Population of London about 145,000.

274

Many theatres built, including
the *Curtain* at Shoreditch and
the *Rose* and the *Hope* on Bankside.

275

The city was at the height of its prosperity.

276

Moorfields was drained and laid out as a pleasure-ground.

277

Wealthier citizens built country houses.

278

Courtiers built mansions in Westminster, Whitehall, the Strand and Lincoln's Inn Fields.

279

A regular water-supply was conveyed from the Thames in leaden pipes.

280

The river was a major highway but drainage and refuse poured into it.

281

Most streets were unmade, foul and muddy.

282

The City became the centre of municipal and commercial life.

283

Suburbs grew into a vast encircling town.

284

Old walls were pulled down and a network of streets were built of brick.

285

Pavements were introduced.

1613

A canal brought water from Hertfordshire.

1642–46

During the Civil War, London was a focal point for the
Parliamentarians: new earthwork fortifications were raised.

1649

Charles I of England executed at the Banqueting Hall of the
Palace of Whitehall before vast crowds.

1653

Cromwell's Commonwealth launched. Jews were allowed to
return to London.

1660

Restoration of monarchy with Charles II as king.
The fashionable court life of the West End
and the commercial life of the City
became separate.

291

1664–66

London hit by the Great Plague.
70,000 deaths from plague registered,
but it is probable that
at least 100,000 perished.

292

1666

The Great Fire in September started in a bakery
in Pudding Lane.

293

1666

The fire lasted almost five days and virtually destroyed the
city at a loss of £11 million.

1666

Almost all the remains of medieval London were destroyed
in the fire that burned the cathedral,
palaces and mansions,
85 churches and 13,000 homes –
but only nine people died.

1666–1711

Sir Christopher Wren played a leading role in
rebuilding the city
and designed more than 51 churches,
including St Paul's Cathedral
(completed 1710).

1671

The Monument was erected to commemorate
the fire.

1694

Bank of England was founded.

1698

The old palace of Whitehall was burnt down.

299

1700–1750

Many hospitals were built, including

Westminster Hospital (1719)

Guy's (1725)

St Bartholomew's (rebuilt 1730–33)

St Thomas's (1732)

the London Hospital (1741)

and the Middlesex Hospital (1745).

300

1738

The Foundling Hospital was instituted and moved

to the present building in 1754.

1738

Westminster Bridge was begun.

1750

Westminster Bridge opened,
the first to span the Thames since
London Bridge in the 900s.

1769

Blackfriars Bridge built.

1753

The British Museum launched in Montagu House.

1758

The houses on London Bridge had been demolished

and soon five of the old city gates

Moorgate

Aldersgate

Aldgate

Cripplegate

and Ludgate

were pulled down.

1762

The Westminster Paving Act
introduced better roads,
more pavements were laid,
people put their names on their doors
and the numbering of houses began.

1765

Silk-weavers' riots.

1768

The Royal Academy launched.

1780
Gordon Riots.

Late 1700s
Newspapers began to appear
Morning Post (1772)
The Times (1788)
Observer (1791)
Morning Advertiser (1794)
and *Globe* (1803).

1799
The Royal Institution founded.

1801

The first census
showed that the total population of
London was 900,000
and of the City, 78,000.

1801

First attempts at steam navigation made on
the Thames.

314

1805

The London docks opened.

They covered 120 acres and cost £4million.

315

1806

Great funeral of Lord Nelson

(buried in St Paul's).

316

1807

Gas first used to light public streets.

1812

Regent's Park created.

1812

A charter granted to the Gas Light and Coke Company.

1816

Vauxhall Bridge opened.

1817

Waterloo Bridge opened.

1819

Southwark Bridge built.

1811

The Mint built.

1813

Regent Street built.

1823

The current British Museum built on the site
of Montagu House.

1824

General Post Office built.

1825–31

The new London Bridge created.

1828

London Zoo opened,
initially housing exotic animals
for eminent scientists to study.
In 1847
the zoo opened its doors to the public.

1834

Old Houses of Parliament destroyed by fire.

1837

The young 18-year-old Queen Victoria began her reign.

1837

Euston was London's first railway station.
It opened on 20 July.
The service from London to Birmingham
consisted of three trains a day.

More stations followed:

Paddington Station opened in 1838.

Fenchurch Street in 1841.

Waterloo in 1848.

Kings Cross in 1852.

Victoria in 1860.

Charing Cross 1864.

St Pancras in 1868.

1838

The Royal Exchange destroyed by fire.

333

1839

The first London telegraph
from Paddington to West Drayton.

334

1840

The new Houses of Parliament begun.

335

1840

The Penny Post introduced.

336

1843

The Thames tunnel from Wapping to Rotherhithe opened.

1847

The new House of Lords completed.

1848

London threatened by the Chartists great revolution, and
extensive preparations were made for defence.

1851

Great international exhibition at Crystal Palace.

1852

The new House of Commons completed.

1852

Wellington's funeral procession watched
by 1.5 milllion people.

1854

The Year of the Great Stink.
The smell of waste in the Thames
forced MPs to desert Parliament.

1856

South Kensington Museum and the
Public Record Office founded.

1856

Big Ben installed.

1861

The first trams arrived.

1862

Second great international exhibition.

Inventions and art were displayed in an exhibition hall that would be used later in the building of Alexandra Palace.

1863

The world's first underground railway built between
Paddington and Farringdon Street.
The initial section of track
ran a distace of 6km (nearly 4 miles).

1866

Metropolitan Fire Brigade begun.

1869

The Holborn Viaduct completed.

350

1870

Thames Embankment completed.

351

1871

Royal Albert Hall opened.

352

1876

First telephone call –
made by Alexander Graham Bell
from Brown's Hotel.

353

1879–1909

Over 1,500 miles of new streets built.

354

1882

New Law Courts opened.

355

1886

First Cruft's Dog Show.

356

1888

Jack the Ripper murdered at least five women.

1890

The first tube train ran.

1892

First Oscar Wilde play, *Lady Windermere's Fan*,
performed in London.

1893

The Imperial Institute opened.

1894

Tower Bridge completed.

1896

National Portrait Gallery open.

1896

Now sufficient motor cars to merit the Highways Act and
the first London-to-Brighton run.

1896

Moving pictures demonstrated in Piccadilly.

364

1898

First escalator in London, in Harrods.

365

1900

Work begins on Aldwych and Kingsway
(opened 1905).

366

1900

Population now 4.5 million.

367

1901

Queen Victoria died after a reign of 63 years.

1903

Opening of Catholic Westminster Cathedral, the only building in the Byzantine style in London.

1903

First London taxi.

1909

Victoria and Albert Museum opened.

1910–11

London buses replaced the horse-drawn omnibus service.

372

1914–18

World War I. 2,500 people died in German air raids.

373

1915

Zeppelin raids on city.

374

1926

General Strike.

375

1931

Dorchester Hotel and Broadcasting
House completed.

376

1934

Battersea Power Station completed.

377

1936

Alexandra Palace transmitted television.

378

1936

Crystal Palace fire. The site of the Great Exhibition in 1851 burned to the ground.

379

1939

Poplulation of Greater London 8.7 million.

380

1939–45

World War II.

30,000 people died

and huge areas of London were destroyed.

381

1941

The Blitz.

382

1946

The first flight departed from Heathrow,

London's busiest airport.

383

1948

Olympic games held at Wembley Stadium.

384

1951

Festival of Britain and the
Royal Festival Hall opened.

385

1952

Smog killed some 4,000 people
(Clean Air Act will arrive in 1956.)

386

1958

Gatwick Airport opened to relieve the
strain on Heathrow.

387

1960s

Swinging London:
The Beatles,
Notting Hill Carnival,
mini-skirts
and Carnaby Street.

388

1965

Funeral of Sir Winston Churchill.

1965

Post Office Tower opened.

1978

Central London Mosque opens in Regent's Park.

1982

Tax-free zone in the East End Docklands created to stimulate development.

1981

Brixton Riots and IRA bombs.

393

1981

The last of London's docks close.

394

1981

Nat West Tower opened, tallest building in Europe.

395

1984

Thames Barrier completed. It can be closed at any time to prevent the flooding of the city by high tides.

396

1986

The London Stock Exchange computerised.

1986

Opening of new Lloyd's building
designed by Richard Rogers.

1986

M25 motorway, circuiting London to
relieve traffic congestion, completed.

1987

The City Airport opened.

400

1990

Population of London had declined
to 6.5 million.

401

1990

Canary Wharf Tower completed.

402

1994

Terminal opened at Waterloo Station
of the Eurostar rail service,
linking Britain with Continental Europe
via the Channel Tunnel.

403

1996

New *Globe* theatre opened on South Bank.

404

1997

Funeral of Princess Diana (married Prince Charles in 1981; divorced 1996). Hundreds of thousands lined London streets and the M1 motorway to salute the cortège.

405

2000

Millennium celebrations at Greenwich.

The original Globe theatre

A BRIEF HISTORY

The Old Fountain in the Minories 1798

SHOPS

406

Up to 60,000 people can be working in Oxford Street
at any one time.

407

Oxford Street has over 300 shops.

408

On a clock over the main entrance of Fortnum and Mason
models of the founders bow to each other hourly.

409

1652

Nicholas Culpeper published his first *Herbal*. You can still
visit Culpeper Herbalists in Covent Garden.

1707

Fortnum and Mason was begun by William Fortnum,
formerly a footman in Queen Anne's household;
orders from the royal household helped establish a
high-ranking clientele.

Now amalgamated as Asprey and Garrard, the Royal
jewellers in Bond Street were until recently
separate firms dating back to
the 18th century.

Asprey and Garrard make many of the diamond pieces worn
by the Oscar stars.

413

Charing Cross Road has the highest concentration of bookshops in London.

414

Foyle's Bookshop has 33 departments.

415

Foyle's monthly literary lunches were launched in 1931 by Christina Foyle, daughter of one of the founders, and are attended by authors and celebrities.

SELFRIDGES

416

Selfridges famous store opened in 1909.

417

Selfridges has eight floors.

418

Selfridges is housed in the largest building ever designed as a single shop.

419

During World War II, a decoder was hidden in the basement of Selfridges so when Churchill telephoned Roosevelt, the call went via the store!

420

Over 90,000 people went into Selfridges on the day it opened.

421

Selfridges has nine passenger lifts.

422

Selfridges has 100 departments.

423

Selfridges first sale was a handkerchief
at 1s.4d. (6.7 pence).

HAMLEY'S

424

Hamley's toy shop
has been flourishing for over 240 years.

425

Hamley's toy shop has seven floors of toys, games,
models and gifts.

426

Hamley's toy shop has a haunted staircase.

LIBERTY'S

427

Liberty's attracted pre-Raphaelite artists such as
Rossetti, Leighton and Burne-Jones
and became linked with Arts and Crafts
and Art Nouveau styles.

428

1875

Arthur Liberty founded Liberty's in Regent Street.

429

1875

Liberty's shop began by selling ornaments, fabrics and
objets d'art from Japan and the Far East.

430

1853

Harrods began as a small grocer's shop opened by
a tea retailer.

431

1884

The present Harrods store was built.

432

Harrods site now covers 20 acres (8.094 hectares).

433

Harrods store has over 5,000 staff.

434

Up to 300,000 customers visit Harrods
store each day.

435

Harrods has 330 departments.

Harrods lifts travel some
50,000 miles (80,465 km)
each year.

When Harrods' first escalator was installed
(near the turn of the century)
brandy was served to passengers who felt faint.

Harrods is the third most popular London attraction for
overseas visitors.

Harrods has seven selling floors.

440

Harrods has its own system of private tunnels and subways connecting the store with its warehouse.

Frosty Way leads to the deep-freeze rooms and Wine Cellar Close to wine stocks. The Lock Up is used to hold shoplifters. A fleet of green electric trolleys runs to and fro under Brompton Road.

441

Harrods has 19 bars, cafés and restaurants.

442

The auction house's first-ever sale was held by founder Samuel Baker in 1744.

When he died, Sotheby's sold the books that Emperor
Napoleon had taken into exile.

Sotheby's has auctioned:
Russian space capsules
a Tyrannosaurus Rex fossil
a piece of 60-year-old wedding cake.

1958
1,400 attended the first Sotheby's evening auction since
the 1700s (including Somerset Maugham,
Anthony Quinn and Kirk Douglas). Seven pictures
(sold in 21 minutes) fetched £781,000.

1989

Sales of Impressionist and Modern art
totalled $1.1 billion in
Sotheby's New York and London.

January 2000

'Sothebys.com' was the first auction house to hold
international art auctions on the Internet.

2001

Sotheby's new London saleroom opened.
The auction room measures 54,000 sq ft (5,017.60 sq m)
or two football pitches).

1990s

Sotheby's sold a book, *The Gospels of Henry the Lion*, for over
£8 million.

UNUSUAL LONDON SHOPS

450

Anything Left-Handed, Brewer Street.

451

The Tin-Tin Shop, Sloane Avenue –
focuses on the Belgian cartoon character.

452

Smith's Snuff Shop, Charing Cross Road.

453

High and Mighty, Knightsbridge,
sells tall and large men's clothes –
up to a 60inch (1.524 m) waistline.

454

The Kite Store, Neal Street.

455

UFO Music, Hanway Street: rock memorabilia,
includes John Lennon's old washboards.

456

James Smith and Sons, New Oxford Street –
sells walking sticks and umbrellas.

MARKETS

There have been wholesale food markets in the city of London since Roman times.

AD 43

Plautus and the Roman legions noted a divers market at Southwark.

500 BC

Billingsgate fish market began when King Belin built a small quay guarded by a water-gate – Belin's Gate.

460

Smithfield and Borough markets remain
on their original sites.

461

Smithfield, Billingsgate, Leadenhall, Borough, Spitalfields
and Covent Garden are the seven original wholesale
markets still in operation.

462

By 1276, Southwark (Borough) market spread over London
Bridge.

463

By the 1300s, Borough market spread into St Saviour's
churchyard. Posts prevented cattle wandering over graves.

1933

By this date no fewer than
42 million heads of celery
were passing through Borough market per year!

Petticoat Lane Market acquired its name from the petticoats
sold here in the 1800s.

1300s

Leadenhall Market
was established on the site of a Roman fort.

1400s

Leadenhall Market was appointed to market foodstuffs by famous mayor, Dick Whittington.

14th-century monks from Westminster claimed an open field, known as 'Convent Garden', for burying their dead. In time they developed a garden and sold surplus produce.

1670

Charles II granted a Royal charter for a market at Covent Garden.

1678

There were 22 shops with cellars at
Covent Garden.

1750

Covent Garden market was notorious for its gambling dens,
brothels and bawdy taverns but
still it expanded.

1974

Covent Garden market was relocated to a
56-acre (22.66-hectare) site south of the
river at Vauxhall.

1829-30

Covent Garden's central market
building cost £70,000.

1860

The Floral Hall opened at Covent Garden.

1871

Covent Garden's Flower Market opened.

1904

The Covent Garden's Jubilee Market opened.

1900
Nearly 1,000 porters
earned 30 to 45 shillings
(£1.50 to £2.25) a week
working at Covent Garden.

Early 1900s
Covent Garden was the setting for
flower girl Eliza Doolittle in
Bernard Shaw's *Pygmalion* and the
musical version, *My Fair Lady*
by Lerner and Loewe.

1962

Sold to the Covent Garden Market Authority
for £3,925,000.

2001

About 4,500 vehicles visit
Covent Garden market daily.

481

2001

Over 1,000,000 tons of goods pass through
Covent Garden every year.

482

900s

First livestock market at Smithfield.

483

1173

'... Smithfield a smoth field where
every Friday there is a celebrated rendezvous
of fine horses to be sold'.

484

Meat has been bought and sold at Smithfield for
over 800 years.

1200s to 1650

Smithfield was a place of public executions, especially
for burning, roasting or
boiling to death religious 'rebels'.

1305

Oxen were sold at Smithfield
for 5s 6d (27.5 pence) each.

1357

The kings of England and France attended a royal
tournament at Smithfield.

1381

During the Peasants' Revolt, Wat Tyler met Richard II at Smithfield and was killed by the Lord Mayor. The dagger used is still in the Fishmongers' Hall.

1554-58

277 supposed heretics were burnt alive
at Smithfield.

1615

Smithfield became a great live-cattle market.
It took nine days to drive a herd of cows or a flock of sheep
from the West Country or Wales to London.

491

1853

277,000 cattle and 1,600,000 sheep
were sold at Smithfield.

492

1868

The new Smithfield Market was completed
at a cost of £993,816.

493

1995

Smithfield Market reconstruction cost over
£70 million.

Smithfield Market covers an area of
10 acres (4.05 hectares).

The Smithfield dog,
bred to drive livestock to market,
is still used in Australia for droving.
It was crossed with the Dingo
in the mid-1800s.

85,000 tons of produce pass through the
market each year.

Old Smithfield terminology

A 'pitcher' would unload a carcass.

The carcass was was then cut and weighed
by a 'shipman'.

When the meat was sold, a 'bumaree' would wheel the
meat out to the customer.
The 'bumaree' transported the meat to the client
on 100-year-old wooden barrows that
could carry up to half a ton (508 kilos)!

BILLINGSGATE

498

Billingsgate market was held in the same place for 1,500 years or more.

499

1400

King Henry IV granted citizens the right to collect tolls and customs at Billingsgate, Cheap and Smithfield.

500

By the 1600s, the bad language of the porters and fishwives had made Billingsgate and swearing synonymous: 'She talked like a fishwife.'

1699

An Act of Parliament made Billingsgate a
'free and open market for the sale of fish
six days in the week
and on Sundays for mackerel
to be sold before and after divine service'.

1699

Live eel could not be sold at Billingsgate.
This was the exclusive right of Dutch fisherman,
moored in the Thames,
granted as a thank-you to the Dutch
for having helped feed
Londoners at the time of the Great Fire.

1850s

Annual inventory of fish sold at Billingsgate:

Salmon – 406,000

Live cod – 400,000

Sole – 97,520,000

Whiting – 17,920,000

Haddock – 2,470,000

Mackerel – 23,520,000

Sprats – 4,000,000 lbs

Fresh herrings – 1,050,000,000

Eels – 9,797,760

Bloaters – 147,000,000

Dried haddock – 19,500,000

Oysters – 495,896,000

Lobsters – 1,200,000

Crabs – 600,000

Shrimps – 498,428,648

1982

The Billingsgate building stood on permafrost – frozen for
50 years. In the cold-store were solid blocks of ice,
15 to 20 feet (4.57 to 6.10 m) deep.

1877

Horace Jones designed a magnificent new Billingsgate
market on Lower Thames Street.

Billingsgate porters used to wear leather hats
secured by hundreds of rivets
and strong enough to bear the 420lbs (190.51 kg)
of frozen fish carried on them.

1962
Billingsgate market moved to the Isle of Dogs.

The same handbell is still rung at 5.30 am to indicate the
start of trading at Billingsgate.

200 tons of fish and seafood are sold daily at Billingsgate.

510
WALTHAMSTOWE

Walthamstow Market is over a mile (1.61 km) long –
the longest street market in Britain.

511
CLUB ROW

Club Row, north of Brick Lane,
was once the haunt of bird and animal traders,
who sold rats as live bait for
dog-fighting pits in East End pubs.

Geoffrey Chaucer

Bernard Shaw

Charles Dickens

Thomas Hardy

FAMOUS PEOPLE

In 1867 the first official London plaques arrived to show where famous people had lived. There are about 700 and most are blue with white lettering

mark the homes of authors such as:

Jane Austen, novelist, at 23 Hans Place SW1

Hilaire Belloc, poet, essayist and historian at 104 Cheyne Walk SW3

Sir Arthur Conan Doyle at 12 Tennison Road SE25

Mark Twain who wrote *Huckleberry Finn* and lived briefly at 23 Tedworth Square SW3

514
GREEN PLAQUES

(set up by Westminster City Council)

include plaques for:

Chopin

John F. Kennedy

Liszt

Mozart

Isaac Newton

Tennyson

Dylan Thomas

Van Gogh

William Wallace

515
CHELSEA

was home to:

George Eliot, author
Cheyne Walk

Alexander Fleming, discoverer of penicillin
20a Danvers Street

Charles Kingsley, author
56 Old Church Street

Sir Robert Scott, explorer
56 Oakley Street

Bram Stoker, author
18 St Leonards Terrace

516

Oscar Wilde

The author and playwright lived in Chelsea, at 34 Tite Street. *A Woman of No Importance* (1893) and *An Ideal Husband* (1895) both premiéred at the *Theatre Royal*, Haymarket, where another plaque marks his life and achievements.

517

A. A. Milne

Children's author A A Milne (1882–1956)
is best known for
Winnie-the-Pooh
and *The House at Pooh Corner.*
He lived at 13 Mallord Street, Chelsea SW3.

518
HAMPSTEAD

has plaques for:

D. H. Lawrence, author
Vale of Health NW3

John Constable, painter
40 Well Walk

Aldous Huxley, author, and **Thomas Huxley**, scientist
16 Bracknell Gardens

John Keats, poet
Keats Grove

519
KENSINGTON

was home to:

Béla Bartók, composer
7 Sydney Place

Kenneth Grahame, author
16 Phillimore Place

Henry James, author
34 De Vere Gardens

James Joyce, author
28 Campden Grove

520

Politician **Jawaharlal Nehru** (1889–1964),
India's first prime minister in 1947,
lived at 60 Elgin Crescent, Notting Hill W11,
while studying for the bar in 1910 and 1912.

521

John Reginald Halliday Christie,
murderer (1899–1953),
lived at 10 Rillington Place,
a run-down cul-de-sac where
at least eight murders were committed 1943–53.
Christie even kept a collection of women's
pubic hair in a tobacco tin.

522

Rillington Place, where murderer Christie lived,
was renamed Ruston Close.
The suicide rate, particularly by hanging,
is very high here.

523
MAYFAIR

was home to:

Frederic Chopin, composer
4 St James Place

George Handel, composer
25 Brook Street

Jimi Hendrix, rock star, 23 Brook Street.
The guitarist & singer lived here from 1968–69.

was also home to:

Charles de Gaulle, French politician and general
4 Carlton Gardens

Emperor Napoleon III
1c King Street

Lord Admiral Nelson
147 New Bond Street

Isaac Newton, scientist
87 Jermyn Street

Florence Nightingale, nurse and reformer
10 South Street

Samuel Taylor Coleridge, poet
71 Berners Street

John Dryden, poet
43 Gerrard Street

Karl Marx, political philosopher
28 Dean Street

Percy Bysshe Shelley, poet
15 Poland Street

Jessie Matthews, the dancer and actress,
took her first dance lessons at
22 Berwick Street, above a pub.

Sir Francis Bacon, author and politician
York House, Strand.

At 69–76 Long Acre,
Denis Johnson is commemorated
for having invented the bicycle.

527

Charles Darwin, scientist and author
of *The Origin of Species*,
lived in Bloomsbury at
110 Gower Street WC1.

528

According to the stories written by
Sir Arthur Conan Doyle,
Sherlock Holmes and Doctor Watson
lived at 221b Baker Street 1881–1904.

529

Above a shoe shop,
45a High Street, St John's Wood, is where
Sir Benjamin Britten lived with singer **Peter Pears**.

530

The famous Abbey Road Music Studios
is renowned for its association with The Beatles
pop group but there is also a plaque to
commemorate its opening by **Sir Edward Elgar**.

Near the Paddington branch of the Grand Union Canal
is an area known as Little Venice.
Poet **Robert Browning** was reminded of Venice
when he lived here and a green plaque in
Warwick Crescent marks the site of
his house overlooking the canal.

A plaque at 287 Kennington Road SE11
marks the house where **Charlie Chaplin** spent several
childhood years with his father.

At 140 Park Lane is a plaque to **Keith Clifford Hall**,
pioneer of contact lenses.

534

A plaque to the actress **Dame Anna Neagle**
and her film-director husband
Herbert Wilcox is on a mansion block at 64 Park Lane,
where they shared a suite overlooking Hyde Park.

535

9 St James's Place has a plaque to **Sir Francis Chichester**,
round-the-world yachtsman and navigator.

536

On Bridge Street, just before Westminster Bridge,
a green plaque commemorates the site
of the world's first traffic lights,
and **John Peake Knight** who invented them.

537

Sir Winston Churchill,
politician and British Prime Minister,
lived at 28 Hyde Park Gate.
He also lived at 34 Eccleston Square SW1
and at Caxton Hall in Caxton Street,
where another plaque commemorates him.

538

At 83 Cambridge Street, near the Tate Gallery,
a plaque commemorates designer **Laura Ashley**.

539

Charles Babbage, computer pioneer (1791–1871), lived at
1 Dorset Street W1. He invented a calculating machine, the
computer's precursor.

Botanist **Joseph Banks** (1743–1820),
who voyaged with James Cook
and helped establish the 300-acre Botanic Gardens at Kew,
lived at 32 Soho Square, London W1.

John Logie Baird, inventor of television,
lived at 3 Crescent Wood Road, Sydenham SE26.
He broadcast the first-ever television programme in Britain
from 132–5 Long Acre WC2 in 1929.

Cookery writer **Mrs Beeton** (1836–65), whose *Book of
Household Management* is still in print today, lived at
513 Uxbridge Road.

543

Captain William Bligh (1754–1817)

lived at 100 Lambeth Road SE1.

He was set adrift in an open boat after his crew on the
Bounty mutinied. Bligh and his fellow sailors survived a
journey of over 3,000 miles to reach the East Indies.

544

Venetian painter **Canaletto** (1697–1768)
lived for a time at 41 Beak Street W1.

545

Author **Wilkie Collins** (1824–89)
lived at 26 Wellington Street WC2.
His most successful novel was *The Woman in White*.
This was also Dickens's residence from 1859–70.

Thomas Crapper,
sanitary engineer and originator of the
siphonic toilet flush, lived at
12 Thornsett Road SE20.
Plumber to royalty, he installed toilets and drains for
Queen Victoria at Sandringham.

Charles Robert Darwin, scientist and author of
The Origin of Species lived at the Biological Science
Building, University College, Gower Street WC1.

Dick Whittington, merchant and Lord Mayor of London
four times, lived at 20 College Hill EC4.

549

As a boy, Dickens lived at
16 Bayham Street, Camden NW1,
but his plaque is now on 141. In 1834 he moved to
Furnival's Inn, High Holborn WC1,
demolished in 1897.
Here Dickens wrote the bulk of *Pickwick Papers*.

550

48 Doughty Street
is the only home of Dickens that still exists and
is now the Dickens House Museum.
Here he finished *Pickwick Papers* and wrote
Oliver Twist and *Nicholas Nickelby*.

In 1839 Dickens moved to
1 Devonshire Terrace
(now an office block at 15–17 Marylebone Road).
Here he wrote many novels including
The Old Curiosity Shop, *Martin Chuzzlewit*,
A Christmas Carol and *David Copperfield*,
and kept his pet raven,
featured in *Barnaby Rudge*.

From 1851–59 Dickens lived in Tavistock House, Tavistock
Square WC1.
Here he wrote *Bleak House*, *A Tale of Two Cities*
and some of *Great Expectations*.
He built a theatre in the garden and often acted.

26 Wellington Street WC2 was Dickens's home
from 1859–70.

Thomas Hardy, novelist and poet (1840–1928) studied
architecture in Adelphi Terrace WC2. He was later to live in
Tooting SW17 and Westbourne Park Villas W2.

Painter and engraver **William Hogarth** (1697–1764)
lived at Hogarth House, Hogarth Lane W4,
his country retreat for 15 years.
When in town, Hogarth lived at 30 Leicester Square, where
many of his well-known works were executed, including
A Rake's Progress.

556

Sigmund Freud (1856–1939) lived at
20 Maresfield Gardens NW3 – now a museum.

557

Actor **Boris Karloff** (1887–1969),
star of *Frankenstein* (1931), spent his early years at
36 Forest Hill Road SE23,
before moving to America.

558

After the failure of the Russian revolution of 1905,
revolutionary **Lenin** (1870–1924)
and his wife stayed at 16 Percy Circus WC1
(now the rear of the Royal Scot Hotel in Kings Cross Road).
He studied at the British Museum.

559

John Keats (1795–1821), poet,
was apprenticed to become a surgeon in
Church Street, Edmonton.
He lived at Wentworth Place
(now Keats House, Keats Grove, in Hampstead)
and reputedly wrote *Ode to a Nightingale*
while sitting under a plum tree in the garden.

560

Prior to becoming Emperor of France,
Napoleon III (1808–73) lived at
1 Carlton Gardens SW1 (1839–40).
While in exile, he lived at 1c King Street, St James's SW1.
He also kept apartments at the *Star and Garter Inn* on
Richmond Hill.

Viscount and Admiral, Nelson (1758–1805)
lived at 147 New Bond Street in 1797
and at 103 in 1798.
The only home Nelson ever actually owned was in
Merton Place SW19, since demolished.
He lived here from 1801–5
with Sir William and Lady Hamilton.

Lady Emma Hamilton diverted part of the
River Wandle to flow through the garden at
Merton Place and renamed it 'The Nile'
in honour of Nelson's great victory.
Nelson's affair with her created a huge scandal.

Lady Hamilton also lived in New Bond Street
in about 1811–13.
She was imprisoned for debt shortly afterwards.

Playwright **Joe Orton** (1933–67) lived at
25 Noel Road, Islington,
with his lover Kenneth Halliwell.
He was murdered by Halliwell,
who was jealous of Orton's success
and tortured by his unfaithfulness.

Peter Sellers, comedian and film star (1925–80)
lived at 10 Muswell Hill Road N6.

Diarist and Secretary to The Admiralty

Samuel Pepys (1633–1703)

described London life in the mid 1600s,

including the Great Plague and the Great Fire.

His coded shorthand was not deciphered until 1825.

He lived at Seething Lane EC3

in Navy Offices later destroyed by fire.

He moved to 12 Buckingham Street WC2,

then to 14 Buckingham Street

and, finally, to fashionable Clapham.

Finnegan's Wake, 2 Strutton Ground, is the pub where the
radio show *The Goons* was first planned by **Harry Secombe**,
Peter Sellers *et al.*

FAMOUS PEOPLE

Orchestral conductor **Sir Malcolm Sargent** (1895–1967),
famous for conducting 'the Proms' concerts, lived and died
atAlbert Hall Mansions, Kensington Gore SW7.

Mary Shelley (1797–1851),
who wrote *Frankenstein*, lived at
24 Chester Square SW1.
She was the second wife of Percy Bysshe Shelley the poet.

Mary and **Percy Shelley**
declared their love for one another over her mother's grave
at St Pancras Old Church, Pancras Road NW1.

Thomas Sheraton (1751–1806),
designer of neo-classical furniture,
lived at 106 (now 103) Wardour Street W1
from 1793–5,
and from 1798–1800
at 98 (now 147).
He never actually lived in Little Chapel Street,
in 1937 renamed Sheraton Street in his honour.

Many books by Martin Amis are set around Ladbroke Grove
where for many years he kept an apartment.

Author and playwright **James Barrie** (1860–1937)
is best known for his children's book and play *Peter Pan*
which begins in London.
Peter Pan was staged at the *Duke of York's Theatre*
every Christmas from 1904–14
and Barrie donated all royalties
to Great Ormond Street children's hospital.

Poet **Elizabeth Barrett Browning** (1806–61)
lived at 99 Gloucester Place W1,
and then at Wimpole Street,
until September 1846 when
she eloped with Robert Browning.

Lord Byron (1788–1824)
became famous overnight when *Childe Harold* was
published in 1812.
The fact that he was lame from birth did not inhibit his
prodigious success with women and, perhaps, men. He
had a scandalous affair with Caroline Lamb, wife of Lord
Melbourne (who later became Prime Minister). She said
that he was 'mad, bad and dangerous to know'.

Crime writer **Dorothy Sayers** (1893–1957)
created the character of Lord Peter Wimsey,
amateur detective.
She is buried in the church gardens of St Anne, Soho,
where she was a churchwarden.

SHAKESPEARE

577

William Shakespeare was playwright, actor and poet
(1564–1616). The British Library houses his first folio. In
1594 Shakespeare's *Comedy of Errors* was
first staged at Grays Inn WC1.

578

In 1601 *Twelfth Night* was produced in the Hall of Middle
Temple EC4. *Blackfriars Playhouse* saw production of many
of Shakespeare's plays, and Shakespeare also acted there.

579

During the 1580s Shakespeare is said to have acted with
Burbage in taverns on the Edgware Road.

In 1603 the King's Companie of Comedians, including Shakespeare, performed many plays at Hampton Court for the pleasure of newly crowned James I.

The Globe, Bankside, built 1598–1609, was used only in the summer. Shakespeare was a shareholder and an actor here. In 1613, canon fired during a performance set the thatch on fire and the theatre was burnt to the ground. It was rebuilt and opened again in 1614.

The Puritans closed Shakespeare's *Globe* in 1642 and it was demolished in 1644. *The Globe* has now been reconstructed at Bear Gardens, Bankside SE1.

Playwright **George Bernard Shaw** (1856–1950) worked as a journalist in London from 1876 and for the Edison Telephone Company. He completed five novels, which were rejected, before he turned his hand to plays.

George Bernard Shaw wrote over 50 plays, including *Arms and the Man* (1894) *The Devils Disciple* (1897) and *Pygmalion* (1905).
He won the Nobel Prize for Literature in 1925.

George Bernard Shaw married Charlotte Payne-Townshend in 1898 on condition that they never had sex, and accordingly the marriage was never consummated.

Author **Anthony Trollope** (1815–82)
worked in the Post Office and introduced
the first pillar-boxes.
His best-known work is *Barchester Towers* (1857).
By the 1860s Trollope was earning an
amazing £4,500 from writing.

6 Gordon Square was home of author **Virginia Woolf**
(1882–1941) one of the leading members of the
Bloomsbury Group and innovator of the modern English
novel. Although married, Virginia had a close romantic
friendship with Victoria Sackville-West.
She suffered bouts of mental illness and finally drowned
herself in the River Ouse.

1907–30

The Bloomsbury Group, a distinguished set of English writers and artists, frequently met in the Bloomsbury area near the British Museum, to discuss artistic and philosophical questions.

The Bloomsbury Group included **E. M. Forster**, **Lytton Strachey**, **Bertrand Russell**, **Aldous Huxley**, **T. S. Eliot** and Fabian writer **Leonard Woolf** and his wife **Virginia Woolf** (who together founded the Hogarth Press in 1917).

590

The Old Curiosity Shop at 13 Portsmouth Street WC2
is reputed to have been the home of **Little Nell** in the
Dickens novel.

591

Fleet Street, erstwhile centre of the newspaper industry, was
the setting for the infamous barber shop
of **Sweeney Todd**.

592

Whitechapel is depicted in many books and films.
Jack the Ripper claimed his five victims
all within one square mile.

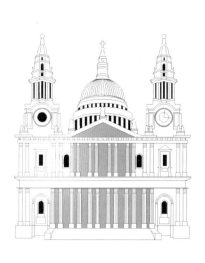

St Paul's Cathedral

BUILDINGS AND MONUMENTS

Banqueting House, Whithall

There are over 18,000 listed buildings in London,
nearly 600 of which are Grade I listed.
21% are within the borough of Westminster.

ROYAL BUILDINGS

Until 1689, British sovereigns used the
Palace of Whitehall as their London residence.
Then they moved to St James's Palace
until 1837 when Queen Victoria
chose Buckingham Palace.

BUCKINGHAM PALACE

595

In 1761 George III purchased Buckingham House
for his wife, Queen Charlotte.
George IV inherited the house in 1820
and it was refurbished and extended.

596

In the courtyard of Buckingham Palace,
the triumphal Marble Arch had been erected to
commemorate British victories at Trafalgar and Waterloo.
Queen Victoria removed it in the 1840s
to make space for a new wing.
The present forecourt was formed in 1911.

When the Houses of Parliament burnt down in 1834,
William IV offered Buckingham Palace
as a new home for Parliament but his offer was declined.

The army's Household Division has guarded the Royal
Family since 1660. Today, the Changing of the Guard
outside Buckingham Palace takes place in a ceremony
lasting around 45 minutes.

Queen Victoria's Buckingham Palace ballroom
was once the biggest room in London,
measuring 122ft (37.19m) long, 60ft (18.29m) wide and
45ft (13.72m) high.

600

Over 50,000 people visit Buckingham Palace every year, as
guests to banquets, lunches, dinners,
receptions and Royal garden parties.
Three garden parties are held each year,
for a total of some 35,000 guests.

BUCKINGHAM PALACE GARDENS

601

One of the palace lakes measures 3 acres. 30 different bird
species are residents or visitors, among them great-crested
grebe, coots, mallard, moorhens,
shelduck and emperor geese –
but a fox caught the flamingos!
Other birds include a tawny owl.

602

Buckingham Palace has the largest private gardens
in London with some 40 acres (16 hectares)
including 20 acres of ornamental grass.

603

Buckingham Palace Gardens are tended by 10 gardeners
with 1 head gardener. There are 29 acres of lawn to mow.
The camomile lawn, the largest cut lawn in Britain,
takes a week to mow.

604

A recent survey discovered 2 new species of fungus in
Buckingham Palace Gardens and some 112 species of spider
include 2 not previously noted in London –
and pipistrelle bats have bred here.

605

James I planted 10,000 mulberry trees to feed silkworms in
Buckingham Palace Gardens.
Trees have often been planted to mark special
Royal Family occasions.
A 1902 copper beech is the oldest of these,
planted by Edward VII and Queen Alexandra
to mark his accession to the throne.

606

The vast Waterloo Vase in Buckingham Palace Gardens
is a 15ft (4.57 m) stone urn, carved from a single block of
Carrara marble, initially commissioned
by Napoleon in anticipation
of his victory over Europe.

ST JAMES'S PALACE

607

St James's was built between 1532–40 by Henry VIII, on the site of the Hospital of St James. For over 300 years it was the primary London royal residence.

608

St James's Palace has housed the London homes of the Prince of Wales (and his offices), Princess Alexandra and her family, the Marshal of the Diplomatic Corps and the Central Chancery of the Orders of Knighthood.

609

The coffin of the late Diana, Princess of Wales, lay in the Chapel Royal in St James's Palace prior to her funeral.

610

Clarence House, formerly home to The Queen Mother, is
located within the grounds of St James's Palace,
as is Lancaster House, used for government
conferences and receptions.

KENSINGTON PALACE

611

William III bought this Jacobean mansion from the
Earl of Nottingham.

612

Queen Victoria was born and raised at Kensington Palace
and heard of her accession to the throne here in 1837.

613

Today, Kensington Palace contains the offices and residences
of Princess Anne,

the Duke and Duchess of Gloucester,

the Duke and Duchess of Kent

and Prince and Princess Michael of Kent.

It was also home to Diana, Princess of Wales.

HAMPTON COURT

614

Hampton Court Palace is situated in the
Royal Borough of Richmond-upon-Thames.

It first came into Royal possession in the 1520s when
Cardinal Wolsey gave it to Henry VIII.

615

George II (reigned 1727–60) was the last reigning monarch
to occupy Hampton Court; in 1851, Queen Victoria
conferred the palace on the British Government.

616

Hampton Court Maze was originally planted in the late
17th century. Famous gardener 'Capability' Brown planted
the current Great Vine in about 1770.

WINDSOR CASTLE

617

Windsor Castle is an official residence of The Queen;
it has been a royal palace and
fortress for over 900 years.

618

In Windsor Castle's State Apartments are many treasures
from the Royal Collection, including paintings
by Holbein, Rubens and Van Dyck.

619

St George's Hall at Windsor Castle has been completely
restored after the fire of 1992
and The Queen holds
state banquets and receptions here.

620

In the Drawings Gallery at Windsor Castle,
old masters include works by
Leonardo da Vinci, Hans Holbein
and Canaletto.

Queen Mary's Dolls' House at Windsor Castle
is the most famous dolls' house in the world,
built to a scale of 1:12
by master craftsmen in the 1920s.

14th-century St George's Chapel
at Windsor Castle is the home of
the Order of the Garter, burial place of
ten sovereigns and scene of many
royal weddings.

THE BANQUETING HOUSE

623

The Banqueting House is the only surviving part of Whitehall Palace, the sovereign's London residence from 1530–1689, before its destruction by fire. Built by Inigo Jones and completed in 1622, The Banqueting House has been used for many state events and banquets.

624

On the 30th January 1649, The Banqueting House was the venue for the execution of Charles I. The head executioner refused to behead his former king and his assistant could not be found. Eventually a hooded individual, whose identity was never revealed, executed the sovereign.

Kew Palace

Kew Palace, set in the grounds of the Royal Botanic
Gardens, was originally bought by George II.
The only monarch to live there was George III,
who was confined to the house from 1802
as doctors tried to cure his 'madness'.

Albert Memorial

The Albert Memorial in Kensington Gardens,
opposite the Albert Hall,
was built in remembrance of Prince Albert,
husband of Queen Victoria,
who died in 1861.

Apsley House

Traditionally the home of the Dukes of Wellington,
Apsley House at Hyde Park Corner originally
had the address of Number One, London.

Bank of England

William III founded the Bank of England in 1694.
Also known as the 'Old Lady of Threadneedle Street',
the bank has occupied its current site since 1734.

BT Tower

Commonly known as the Post Office Tower, in the 1960s
this was the tallest building in London.

Cenotaph

This takes its name from the Greek *kenotaphion*
meaning 'empty tomb'.
It was built in 1919–20 by Edwin Lutyens to
commemorate those lost in the Great War.

Centrepoint

On the corner of Charing Cross Road
and New Oxford Street,
this imposing skyscraper is built
on the site of a notorious slum
called St Giles.

Charing Cross

Twelve memorials were erected by Edward I
(who ruled 1272–1307)
to mark the resting places of his wife's funeral cortège
as her body travelled south from Nottingham.
The original Charing Cross was pulled down by
Roundheads during the Civil War
and today's Charing Cross
(outside the station with the same name)
is a Victorian replica.

633

Child's Bank

Set in Fleet Street, this is the oldest bank in Britain,
dating from 1559.

634

Cleopatra's Needle

London's oldest monument has no connection
with the Egyptian queen and was originally erected
in Heliopolis in around 1475 BC.
The Turkish viceroy of Egypt presented it to Britain in
1819 but it did not arrive here until 1878.

635

Constitution (or Wellington) Arch

This stands in the centre of Hyde Park Corner
and in 1828 commemorated
Britain's victories in the Napoleonic Wars.
The Arch was originally a gateway into the
grounds of Buckingham Palace.

636

Eros

The cherub-like statue at Piccadilly Circus is officially
entitled 'The Angel of Christian Charity' and was erected in
1893 as a memorial to the social and industrial reformer,
7th Earl of Shaftesbury.

637

The Guildhall

The first Guildhall was built in the early 1400s,
but was virtually destroyed by the Great Fire of 1666.
Today's Guildhall was largely built in 1673.
The Great Hall is 150ft (46m) long and 50ft (15m) wide.
In 1987, the remains of a Roman amphitheatre were found
close to the Guildhall.

Houses of Parliament

The Palace of Westminster was the site of a
royal palace for 1,000 years.
A palace was built for Edward the Confessor
in the 11th century. By 1550,
this was being used by Parliament but in
1834 was devastated by a fire.
The present buildings were completed in 1860.

Lloyds Building

This striking office block in Leadenhall Street,
built in 1984 and designed by Richard Rogers,
is the headquarters for Lloyds Bank.

The London Stone

This block of limestone, located outside an office block in
Cannon Street, is an ancient monolith. During the Kentish
Revolt of 1450, rebel Jack Cade struck it as he declared
himself Lord of the City.

Marble Arch

Marble Arch marks the western tip of Oxford Street.
This was the site of the notorious gallows at Tyburn,
the city's main place of execution from 1300 to 1783.
Public hangings were a popular event
and on more than one occasion
the stands collapsed under the
weight of massive crowds.

The Monument

Designed by Sir Christopher Wren,
this commemorates the Great Fire of London.
It took six years to construct, from 1671 to 1676.
Folklore has it that if laid on its side,
the Monument would identify
the exact spot where the fire began.
The balcony is reached by a spiral staircase
with 311 steps.

643

Peter Pan

The much-loved monument in Hyde Park was erected in
1912 using funds donated by the author J. M. Barrie,
who walked in the park regularly.

Queen's House

This stands on Tower Green and was originally a prison.
Three English queens were incarcerated here:
Catherine Howard, Anne Boleyn and Lady Jane Grey.

645

Seven Dials

Between Covent Garden and Shaftesbury Avenue
is the curiously-named Seven Dials area
named after a Doric pillar topped by a seven-faced clock set
at the junction of several roads in 1694 –
which was a regular meeting place for local villains.
The pillar was removed in 1773 but Queen Beatrix of the
Netherlands had a new column erected here in 1989.

Somerset House

Edward Seymour built the first
Somerset House in 1547.
After the Civil War, it was occupied by the army and Oliver
Cromwell's body was stored here.
Somerset House was rebuilt in 1809
and has been used by
the Register of Births, Deaths and Marriages
and the Inland Revenue.
Now, after a £48million refurbishment,
it has museums, restaurants and shops.

TOWER OF LONDON

647

The Tower of London was begun shortly after
William the Conqueror's invasion of England and The
White Tower was completed around 1078.

648

The Tower of London has been used as:

a palace

a prison

an arsenal

a royal mint

a place of execution

a zoo

and a public records office.

The Tower was a place of execution from the Middle Ages.
Among those dispatched here were Anne Boleyn in 1536
and Lady Jane Grey in 1554. In 1483,
Edward V and his young brother were last seen in the Tower
before they disappeared,
presumed murdered. In 1674,
two children's skeletons, thought to be the princes',
were discovered in the Bloody Tower.

650

Resident ravens have nested at the Tower
since the 1600s.
Tradition has it that the State will fall should
the ravens ever desert the Tower.

Trafalgar Square

This most famous of London's squares
was constructed on the site of the King's Mews
and took 20 years to complete.
The square commemorates Britain's naval victory
at the Battle of Trafalgar.

Nelson's Column is 185ft (56m) high
topped by a 17ft (5m)
statue of Admiral Nelson.
Four lions sculpted by Landseer guard the base.

653

The Thames Barrier, between Silvertown on the
north bank and Woolwich on the south,
was completed in 1982,
at a cost of £500 million,
and is the world's largest movable flood barrier.

654

The Thames Barrier has been raised more than 20 times to
protect London from flooding.
When raised, each of the 4 main gates is the height of a
5-storey building.

655

The Thames Barrier can be closed within 30 minutes.
The gates turn through 90° to stand
52 ft (15.85m) above the river bed.

LONDON EYE

656

Riding the Eye

The London Eye has 32 passenger capsules,
each of which can carry 25 people –
15,000 visitors a day.
Passengers can see over 25 miles –
as far as Windsor Castle.

The London Eye is the world's largest observation wheel at
443ft (135m), nearly 3 times the height of Tower Bridge.
1,700 tons of steel were used in its construction.
London's fourth tallest structure,
it weighs 2,100 tons.
It took over a week to lift it from a horizontal
to a vertical plane.
It rotates an average 6,000 times a year.
Each revolution takes 30 minutes.

658

The Eye's Revolution
The Eye turns continuously at 25% of walking speed
10.24ins (26 cm) per second.

THE MILLENNIUM DOME

659

The Millennium Dome's roof at 20 acres
(8.09 hectars), is the biggest roof in London.

Its enclosed volume is 2.1 million cubic metres –
equivalent to 3.8 billion pints or
12.8 million barrels of beer.

It is the largest ever fabric construction, with
1 million sq ft (28,317 sm) of material, so strong it could
support the weight of a jumbo jet.

If it was inverted and put under Niagara Falls
it would take 10 minutes to fill.

The Dome's 'footprint' is
10 times the size of St Paul's Cathedral.
The area it covers is . . .
100 times larger than Stonehenge
3 times larger than Rome's Coliseum
25 times larger than the Taj Mahal.

661

Canary Wharf

The name derives from earlier dockland days, when many
imports came from the Canary Islands.
Construction work commenced in May 1998 to include
office buildings, multi-level shopping facilities, and the
Docklands Light Railway station.

One Canada Square

The tower at Canary Wharf has 50 floors and is 800 feet
(244 metres) high – the tallest building in Britain.
Some 7,000 people work there.
It takes the lifts 40 seconds to travel from the lobby
to the 50th floor.

663

One Canada Square is designed to sway nearly
14 inches (356mm) in the strongest winds.
An aircraft warning light at the top of the tower flashes 40
times a minute – 57,600 times a day.

Burning at the stake

GRIM LONDON

Hanging

AD **60**

When Boadicea attacked Roman London, up to 70,000
died. One myth holds that Boadicea is buried under
King's Cross railway station.

1087

The first recorded case of leprosy in Britain was the Bishop
of London. Lepers were banned from the City and St James's
Palace became a lepers' hospital.

1189

Riots led to looting and buildings being set alight;
30 Jews were killed.

Thieves who stole gold and jewels from the treasure-house
of Westminster Abbey were executed and flayed. Their
tanned skins were used to cover a door, which still leads
from the monks' cloisters.

1212

When fire broke out on London Bridge, 3,000 people died,
burned in their wooden houses there.

1300

Hangings took place at Tyburn
(where Marble Arch now stands) from 1300–1783.

670

1305

Scottish hero William Wallace was hanged, disembowelled, beheaded and quartered at Smithfield.
His head was boiled and preserved with tar, and was the first to be displayed on London Bridge.

671

1530

A poisoner called Rose (or Roose)
was boiled alive at Smithfield.

672

1538

A prior was roasted to death in a cage for refusing to accept Henry VIII's religious supremacy.

673

1349

The Black Death, pneumonic and bubonic plague
killed about 30,000, half London's population.

674

The Devil Tavern (later the *Prospect of Whitby*)
pub at Wapping Wall was the haunt of smugglers,
thieves and men who dragged bodies
from the river to sell to medical schools.

675

1447

Five men were to be hanged, drawn and quartered.
Just as they reached the disembowelling stage,
they were reprieved but had to walk home naked.

1600s

The pirate flag, the Skull and Crossbones,
was adopted from a stone skull and crossed bones
in the grounds of St Nicholas Church,
Deptford Green,
known as the sailors' church.

1701

Pirates, including Captain Kidd,
were executed outside *The Devil Tavern*
at Execution Dock.
They were hanged for 30 minutes then
chained to a stake in the river for 3 high tides.

678

A derrick crane is named after the gallows
devised by hangman Derrick,
who was himself sentenced to death.
The Earl of Essex reprieved him but his
gratitude did not prevent Derrick from
later beheading the earl in 1601.

679

The word 'bedlam', meaning noisy violent chaos,
comes from the Bethlehem Royal Hospital,
a home for the mentally ill since medieval times.
Inmates were chained in cells, and from the 1600s,
sightseers paid to view them.

1661

After the Restoration, the bodies of Parliamentary leaders

Cromwell, Bradshaw and Ireton

were dug up and dragged to Tyburn

to be hanged in their shrouds and then decapitated.

Their heads were set outside Westminster Hall for nearly

20 years until blown down in the wind.

1664–66

The Great Plague

An outbreak in 1625 killed about 40,000.

A new outbreak, spread by fleas on rats,

killed about 75,000 Londoners in 1664–66.

Plague pits

Bodies of plague victims were hastily thrown into pits.
Blackheath probably derived its name
from the plague pit there.
Liverpool Street Station is built on the
site of another plague pit.

1685

At Tower Hill, executioner Jack Ketch
(whose name became a nickname for future hangmen) took
three swings to behead the Duke of Monmouth,
whose head was sewn back so that a portrait
could be painted.

1709–25

Tyburn gallows were large enough for 21 people to be
hanged at the same time,
while the public watched from galleries.
In 1724 a record 200,000 saw
handsome Jack Sheppard hanged.

1772

Thief John Haynes was hanged at Tyburn
in 1772 and his body sold to a
hospital for experiments.
He woke up on the dissection table,
and had to be executed again.

1807

Public executions attracted large crowds.
When a pie seller fell over in a crowd of 40,000,
nearly 100 spectators died in the ensuing chaos.

687

1820

The Cato Street Conspirators plotted to murder
the entire government.
Betrayed and arrested after a fight in
which a Bow Street officer was killed,
the five ringleaders were the last men hanged
and then beheaded at Newgate.
The executioner used a surgeon's knife.

1840

Sweeney Todd

The demon barber who slit his customer's throats
was supposed to be based at 186 Fleet Street.
According to the story, his neighbour,
Mrs Lovett, made meat pies from the bodies
and sold them in nearby Bell Yard.

1842

At least six people killed themselves
by jumping off the Monument
before its rooftop gallery was fenced.

1857

80,000 prostitutes worked the London streets
that had 6,000 brothels.

1858

During the Great Stink, the smell from the Thames grew so
strong that Parliament had to close and later agreed to build
proper sewers.

1867

A total of 276 infant bodies found abandoned in London,
floating in ponds or left in dustholes,
churches, cellars and cesspits.

1875

Wainwright had killed his mistress and was moving her
chopped-up body from a warehouse in Whitechapel Road.
A man who helped load the parcels into a cab
became suspicious and ran after the cab,
calling for a policeman.

1888

Jack the Ripper killed at least six prostitutes
in Whitechapel.
He cut their throats, mutilated their bodies
and then sent taunting letters to the police –
and half a human kidney.

695

1898

George Chapman took out new pub tenancies with
three successive wives, each of whom he poisoned.

696

1910

Dr Crippen poisoned his wife at
39 Hilldrop Crescent, Lower Holloway,
burned the bones and buried parts of her in the cellar before
fleeing by ship to Canada with his lover.
He was the first murderer to be caught by wireless,
as the captain alerted British police
and they in turn alerted
the US authorities.

697

1914

Brides in the bath

Murderer George J. Smith killed his third wife at
14 Bismarck Road (now Waterlow Road). As with his first
two wives, the motive was to claim insurance money and he
drowned her – as he had drowned the others –
in the bath.

698

November 1917

At 101 Charlotte Street (now Astor College),
butcher Louis Voison killed his estranged wife.
Her trunk was found in Regent Square,
her legs in another parcel nearby,
and her head in an outbuilding.

1940s–50s

At 10 Rillington Place, John Christie assaulted and killed at
least seven women, including his wife, hiding their bodies
around the house. Christie put the blame on lodger
Timothy Evans, who was hanged in 1948. In 1953
another body was discovered, and Christie was hanged.

700

1940

In the Blitz that began in September 1940
about 18,000 tons of bombs were dropped
in 71 major raids in 6 months.
Over 20,000 Londoners were killed.

1960s

The Kray Twins ran London's major criminal gang
during the sixties.

In 1966, Ronnie shot a rival gang member
in the *Blind Beggar* pub, Whitechapel Road.

A would-be informer is rumoured to be buried in
a concrete support of the Hammersmith Flyover.

1978

On Waterloo Bridge,
Bulgarian exile Markov,
was killed by a hypodermic needle concealed
in an umbrella.

1981–83

Workmen clearing drains in Muswell Hill discovered a
blockage caused by human remains.
Dennis Nilsen had killed at least three men.
He buried some parts, threw some away
and flushed others down the drains.
He had already claimed at least twelve other
victims while living in Cricklewood.

GRIM MUSEUMS

The London Dungeon

A museum near London Bridge
has exhibits on murders, execution and torture.

Madame Tussaud's

Madame Tussaud started her collection of wax models in the 1790s when, after the French Revolution, she was forced to model victims of the guillotine.

The Chamber of Horrors has many gruesome exhibits.

GHOSTS

Smithfield Market is haunted by a ghost who steals joints of meat

GHOSTS
282

Adelphi arches

In the vaults between the
Strand and the Thames is Jenny's Hole,
haunted by the ghost of a poor prostitute
strangled there in 1875.
Her ragged figure disappears into the walls
but muffled screams linger in the air.

Adelphi Theatre, Strand

Actor-manager William Terriss was stabbed to death
by an unstable actor in 1897 outside the stage door.
Ever since, his tall presence has been sensed.
Some hear his tapping walking stick
or see glowing lights.

Albery Theatre, St Martin's Lane

The handsome ghost of its founder,
Sir Charles Wyndham, crosses the empty stage and
disappears into the dressing-rooms.

Amen Court, near St Paul's Cathedral

A dark shape crawls along the top of the old wall
and the rattle of chains is heard.
Cat-burglar Jack Sheppard escaped
from Newgate Prison and over the
wall of Amen Court three times,
despite being loaded with chains.
He was hanged in 1724.

228 Baker Street

Actress Sarah Siddons haunts the site of her old home, now
an electrical substation.

Bank of England

Sarah Whitehead, the Black Nun,
used to make daily visits to the Bank to ask if her
brother was working there.
He had been put to death for forgery.
She was buried in the graveyard,
later the Bank's gardens, and her black-clad
form still wanders the grounds.

Bank of England

An 18th-century cashier,
nearly 8ft tall,
was terrified of body-snatchers
and so his coffin was buried inside the Bank.
His huge ghost stalks the corridors at night.

Blackwall Tunnel

In 1972, a motorcyclist gave a boy a lift
from the south end of this Victorian tunnel
but his passenger had vanished when
he reached the other end.
He went to the address the boy had given but
found that the lad had died many years before.

714

Bell Lane, Enfield

A phantom coach, running six feet above the ground,
lurches out of the darkness here.

715

50 Berkeley Square

In the 1870s, two sailors broke into the empty house.
In the night banging noises and footsteps disturbed their
sleep. Then the appearance of an oozing mass made one
sailor flee. The other fell to his death out of the window.

716

Buckingham Palace

A ghostly gunshot is supposedly the echo of the suicide of
Edward VII's private secretary.

Black Swan, Bow Road

The cellar is haunted by sisters Cissie and Sylvia Reynolds,
who died when a Zeppelin bomb destroyed the pub in
1916.

Broadcasting House, Portland Place

A butler carrying a tray limps along the
3rd and 4th floor corridors and is often taken
for a real waiter – until he disappears.

Buckingham Street

Samuel Pepys lived for 12 years at No. 12,
and in 1953 a resident saw his smiling ghost here.

Buckingham Palace

A monk, bound in chains, sometimes appears on the great
terrace on Christmas Day. He is believed to have died in a
prison cell when a priory stood on the site.

Bush Theatre, Shepherd's Bush

The ghost of poet Dylan Thomas has been seen at the back
of the theatre, once the BBC rehearsal rooms he used.

Chiswick Police Station

Sounds of a woman moving around the basement are heard
at the site of a cellar where, in 1792, a woman was
butchered by her son-in-law.

Cleopatra's Needle

There are more suicide attempts here than on any other stretch of the Thames. The Needle is associated with a tall naked figure who disappears over the wall into the river but makes no splash.

Cleopatra's Needle

A frantic young woman begged a police officer
to help someone in trouble.
She led him to Cleopatra's Needle,
where he was just in time to stop a
woman throwing herself into the river.
The lady who had fetched him vanished before he
recognised the woman he rescued as the same person.

Coliseum Theatre

The ghost of a World War I soldier walks down
the dress-circle aisle just before the performance begins; he
made his first spectral appearance on
3 October 1918, the day he was killed.
He had spent his last night on leave in this theatre.

Covent Garden Underground

When the station has closed for the night,
a phantom in old-fashioned clothes
and white gloves is sometimes seen
by staff, and footsteps are heard in
the tunnels and on the stairs.

Croydon Airport

The airport is haunted by:

A Dutch pilot who crashed here in bad weather.

Three nuns who died in an aeroplane fire.

A wartime pilot who rides his motorbike over the airfield.

Eaton Place

In June 1893,

the figure of Admiral Sir George Tryon,

in full naval uniform, walked through a party

his wife was holding.

He was, in fact, lying dead in his ship after a

collision at sea in the Mediterranean.

Durward Street

A misty figure is seen lying motionless in the gutter where
Jack the Ripper's first victim was found murdered.

Green Park

This leper burial site was a popular spot for duels in the
1700s. At dawn, the sounds of duelling can sometimes be
heard with panting breath and the clashing of swords.

Green Park

Harsh talking, evil laughter and agonised moans
emanate from a tree where a tall,
staring figure is sometimes glimpsed.

Greyfriars Churchyard

is haunted by:

A monk from the 1200s.

King Edward II's wife, Isabella of France (the 'She-wolf'),
who died in 1358.

Elizabeth Barton, the 'Holy Maid of Kent',
executed in 1534.

Lady Alice Hungerford, executed at Tyburn for poisoning
her husband.

The Gun Inn, **Docklands**

Admiral Horatio Nelson has been seen in this pub,
where he often met his mistress Lady Hamilton.

Hammersmith Graveyard

A white figure appears amongst the tombstones.
One woman, chased by the figure, later died of shock.
A ghost-hunter, lying in wait one night,
shot and killed an innocent passer-by in white overalls.

Hampstead Heath

A ghostly rider, galloping on a black horse,
is believed to be highwayman Dick Turpin.
Hoofbeats, heard suddenly in the middle of the night
outside *The Spaniards* pub, are said to be those of
Turpin's horse, Black Bess.
Turpin often stayed at the inn.

Hampton Court

Catherine Howard, Henry's VIII's fifth wife,
runs screaming down the Haunted Gallery to the
Royal Closet where Henry was at mass
in 1542 when when she learnt
she was to be executed.
The ghost of Cardinal Wolsey, who built the palace,
has also been seen.

Highgate Cemetery

An old woman roams the tombs.
A white, shrouded figure with bony fingers lurks
near the main gates.
The cemetery is said to be the home of a vampire.

Holland House, Holland Park

This was home to a headless ghost and to 'doppelgangers'.
Female members of the family were said to meet themselves
in the house shortly before they died.

Holland House, Holland Park

Sir Henry Rich, first Earl of Holland, was beheaded in
1649, and his ghost is sometimes seen at midnight,
holding his head in his hand.

Horn Inn, Crucifix Lane

A crying child is heard; meanwhile, the ghost of an old lady
moves furniture around and sleeps in empty beds.

Imperial War Museum

Parts of the building were originally the Bethlehem Royal
Hospital (Bedlam) for the insane. Groans, shrieks and
rattling chains disturbed the sleep of World War II
auxiliaries barracked there.

Imperial War Museum

The old Bedlam site is haunted by
the unhappy figure of Rebecca,
who died in the 1700s
and is still searching
for a gold sovereign stolen from her,
the gift of a lover who had deserted her.

Isle of Dogs

The names of this peninsular,
and neighbouring Barking,
derive from a huntsman and his bride drowned in the mud
on a wedding-day boar hunt here.
A skeletal horseman and a pack of hounds
are seen at nights.

Kensington Palace

When strong winds blow,
the pale face of mortally ill King George II
can be seen at a window, staring at the weather-vane.

Ladbroke Grove

A phantom bus used to speed by, with lights on but
no driver or conductor, causing crashes and accidents as
motorists swerved to avoid it – and then vanishing.
Witnesses reported how cars swerved on an apparently
empty road. Now the dangerous corner has been made
safer and the bus no longer roars past.

Lambeth Palace

A phantom of the barge that took Anne Boleyn
to the Tower in 1536 is seen on the river outside
the palace water tower.

Lambeth Palace

At the door of the Undercroft in the palace crypt,
a woman's pleading voice is believed to be that of Anne
Boleyn, begging Archbishop Cranmer not to have
her executed for adultery.

The London Palladium, Argyll Street

A woman in a crinoline haunts
the Crimson Staircase behind the Royal Circle.

749

New Scotland Yard

Although the police HQ has moved, the headless figure of a woman still haunts the site. It is believed to be the ghost of a woman whose body was discovered when the police offices were built. Her head was never found.

749

The Old Burlington, Chiswick

A ghost wearing a wide-brimmed black hat and a long cloak haunts this pub where highwayman Dick Turpin drank.

750

The Old Queen's Head, Islington

Built by Sir Walter Raleigh – and haunted by a young lady in a long, rustling dress who is heard running upstairs.

The Old Vic, Waterloo Road

The ghost of an distraught woman,
wringing her bloody hands, is believed by some to be an
actress who played Lady Macbeth.

Pond Square, Highgate

The Pond Square chicken
was the world's first frozen poultry.
In 1626 Francis Bacon wanted to test whether snow acts
as a preservative. Stopping his coach, he had a local chicken
killed and plucked, then stuffed the carcass with snow.
Bacon collapsed in the cold, and died soon afterwards. Ever
since, the featherless bird has
been seen here, squawking in fear.

754

Ratcliff Wharf

In 1971, building workers saw an old man
in dated clergyman's clothes,
and then watched him disappear.
200 years ago, lodgers here were rumoured to have been
murdered for their money by their host,
the Vicar of Ratcliff Cross.

755

Red Lion Square, Holborn

The garden square is visited by three ghosts, who walk from
south to north diagonally, talking together.
These may be Parliamentary leaders Cromwell, Ireton and
Bradshaw, whose corpses were dug up and taken
to the gallows in Red Lion Fields.

St Bartholomew's Church

The cowled figure of its 1123 founder haunts the church,
preaching to an invisible congregation.
He usually appears at 7am on 1 July.

St Bartholomew's Church

The ghost of painter Hogarth, who frequented the
church, is also seen.

St Bartholomew's Church

Outside the gate was the execution site of Smithfield.
Passers-by sometimes smell burning flesh or hear screams
and groans, or the crackle of burning wood.

St James's Church, Garlick Hill

In 1839, the embalmed body of a young medieval
man was found in a glass coffin during excavations –
Britain's only known example of embalming.
A priest, fireman, church visitors and a young boy
have all seen his white-shrouded form walking here.

St Paul's Cathedral

A whistling figure in old-fashioned clerical clothes
used to appear in a chapel here and then
vanish into the stonework.
During repairs, a secret door leading to a staircase to the
dome was found where the ghost disappeared.

St James's Park

Pedestrians, motorists and members of the Coldstream
Guards barracked nearby have seen a headless woman
in a blood-splattered white-and-red striped dress
run towards the lake.
She was first seen in the early 1800s, some years after a
soldier at the barracks killed his wife and threw her
headless body into the canal that used to be here.

St Magnus the Martyr, London Bridge

A robed and cowled figure has been seen several times
in the church but the figure just fades away
and disappears.

St Thomas's Hospital

A Grey Lady wearing a pre-1920s nurse's uniform is often
seen, but only from mid-calf upwards;
she walks on floors now replaced at a higher level.
She is often seen by patients, and cares for them
before the real nurses arrive.

Thomas à Becket, Old Kent Road

Built on the site of a gallows, this boxers' pub is known for
frightening disturbances. Some publicans would never
sleep alone there. One customer sneered at the idea but the
next minute his beer glass burst in his hand.

Sadler's Wells Theatre

The ghost of Joe Grimaldi, the well-known clown,
has been seen here at night, in his full make-up,
sitting in one of the boxes.

The Strand

The elderly figure of philanthropist
Baroness Burdett-Coutts (of the Coutts banking family),
who died in 1906,
has been seen in Edwardian dress,
walking in broad daylight along the Strand.
She has also been seen in Bethnal Green
where she helped with many charitable donations.

767

Smithfield

The ghost of a gentleman wearing a lawyer's gown
used to appear in Smithfield Market on Saturday nights and
raid butcher's stalls, taking joints of meat.

768

Somerset House

On clear mornings, Admiral Nelson may be seen walking
across the quadrangle towards the Old Admiralty Office.

769

Temple

The ghost of Sir Henry Hawkins has been seen gliding
through the cloisters in wig and gown,
a bundle of papers under his arm.

Theatre Royal, Drury Lane

The Man in Grey has been seen by actors,
staff and audience.
He appears in daytime in the upper circle,
often in the 1st seat of the 4th row, then walks along the
gangway to disappear into the wall by the Royal Box.
He wears riding boots, a white wig, a sword and
carries a tricorn hat.
In the 1800s, workmen found a skeleton
with a 1600s dagger lodged between its ribs
in a small room bricked up at the exact spot where
the ghost disappears.
The ghost is a good omen:
if he is seen in the early
days of a production, it will be a success.

Theatre Royal, Dury Lane

Ghosts include:

Dan Leno (a comedian who reappears in his favourite
dressing room).

Actor-manager Charles Kean, who died in 1868.

King Charles II plus retinue.

TOWER OF LONDON

No place in London is more haunted than the Tower. Ghosts
include headless women,

processions,

a man on a stretcher with his head tucked in the crook of
his arm, and a giant bear.

The huge shadow of an axe has been seen on the
wall of the White Tower.
Two small figures in white nightgowns are believed
to be the Princes murdered in the Tower in 1483.

Thomas à Becket was once Constable of the Tower of
London. His ghost was first seen here in 1241, possibly the
earliest recorded sighting of a ghost in England.

In 1972, a 9-year-old tourist saw an execution scene
re-enacted before her, and correctly told her family that
Anne Boleyn had been beheaded by sword, not axe.

Tower of London

Screams and moans have been heard
coming from the main floor of the White Tower
where prisoners were tortured.
Groans and the squeaking of torture instruments are also
heard in the Council Chamber of the Queen's House where
Guy Fawkes was tortured.

Tower of London

Sir Walter Raleigh haunts Raleigh's Walk,
a path along the ramparts by the Bloody Tower where he
often walked by day when imprisoned in 1604.
On moonlit nights, Raleigh may also be seen
strolling along the path.

Tower of London

In 1864, under the room where Anne Boleyn awaited her execution, a guard at the door of the Lieutenant's Lodgings saw a white-draped figure. He charged at it with his bayonet but fainted when he met only thin air. Major General Dundas witnessed this from a window in the Bloody Tower. Field Marshal Lord Grenfell confirmed he had seen the ghost several times.

University College

The clothed skeleton of philosopher Jeremy Bentham is on display in the college lobby, as requested in his will. His ghost has been seen, with white gloves and walking stick, tapping his way around the college.

University College

Patients and nurses have seen a phantom nurse,
widely held to be Lizzie Church who accidentally killed her
fiancé with a morphine overdose.

Walpole House, Chiswick Mall

Barbara Villiers, Duchess of Cleveland, died here,
fat and bloated. A great beauty when young,
and mistress of Charles II until he met Nell Gwynne,
she always wore high heels.
The clicking of her shoes is heard
and she is seen pleading to the heavens,
supposedly for the return of her beauty.

Vine Street Police Station, Piccadilly

Heavy footsteps, locked cell doors found opened
and papers scattered in empty offices are said to be the acts
of a police sergeant who committed suicide
in a cell in the early 1900s.

Westminster Abbey

A Benedictine monk, known as Father Benedictus,
has spoken to visitors, once saying that he was
killed in the reign of Henry VIII.
Three visitors reported that the figure walked
about an inch (25 mm)
above stones worn down over the ages.

784

The Volunteer, Baker Street

Rupert Nevill, wearing breeches and fancy stockings, haunts the cellar of this pub on the site of the Nevill house that burnt down in 1654.

785

Wimbledon Common

Highwayman Jerry Abershaw, hanged in 1795, still gallops across the common at night.

786

Westminster Abbey

Spectral priests – singly and in procession (once seen by a policeman) – walk through the Abbey to disappear through closed doors.

787

Westminster Abbey

A mud-stained soldier in World War I khaki uniform makes brief appearances by the tomb of the Unknown Warrior.

788

Westminster Abbey

The footsteps of a midnight walker in the Abbey Deanery are believed to be John Bradshaw's. It was here that he pronounced sentence of death on King Charles I.

789

Ye Olde Gate House, Highgate

A black-robed figure haunts the gallery of this 1300s pub, but only when there are no children or animals present.

Farringdon Street and the Fleet Prison

LONDON POLICE AND PRISONS

late 1200s

The Mayor launched a campaign against crime,
including the revival of a curfew.

1200s

A night and day guard called the Watch and Ward protected
the City.

1663

A body of paid nightwatchmen was
established in the City.

1718

An Act made transportation to
America or the West Indies
the most common punishment for serious crimes.

The Old Bailey courthouse stands on the site
of the infamous Newgate Prison.
In the 1700s it was the busiest
criminal court in England.

The Bow Street Runners were set up in 1750, named after
the new courthouse in Bow Street.

1786

A new penal colony was set up in
Botany Bay, Australia,
after fears of a crime wave in London
as transportation to America ended.

1798–1800

A police force was set up to
deter piracy on the Thames,
particularly around the docks.
It was the forerunner of the Marine Police Force.

1805

A Horse Patrol of 60 men was created
to rid the main roads of highwaymen
within a 20-mile radius of the City.

1829

Sir Robert Peel founded
the Metropolitan Police Force (the Met).

1838

The Bow Street Runners
and the Marine Police
were both incorporated into the Met.

LONDON POLICE AND PRISONS

1839

The City of London Police Force was established.

1864

Tunics and helmets replaced
swallow-tail coats and top hats.

1864

The new drop gallows
had been introduced at Newgate
and five pirates were hanged side by side.

1890

New Scotland Yard,
the headquarters of the Metropolitan Police, was opened.

1894

Fingerprinting came into operation in London.

The 'Black Maria' is the nickname for police vans with
locked cubicles that transport prisoners.
The name derives from a powerful
black lodging-house keeper called Maria Lee who,
in the 1830s, helped police in Boston
to escort drunks to the cells.

LONDON POLICE AND PRISONS

807

100 years ago,
only men aged over 21 and under 27
could join the Metropolitan Police.

808

Police boxes

The large blue kiosks,
topped with a flashing light and
linked by phone to the local police station,
arrived in the 1920s.
In the 1960s they were replaced by personal radios.
Fictional Time Lord, Doctor Who,
used a police box as his
Tardis time machine.

Dialling 999

The 999 telephone emergency service
was first introduced in 1937.

PRISONS

Fleet Prison

This was founded in 1197
and was accessible by road and the Fleet River
(now built over).
It was virtually destroyed three times:
in the Peasants' Revolt of 1381;
in the Great Fire of 1666;
and in the Gordon Riots of 1780.

811

Fleet Prison: mid-1700s

The prison was used mainly to incarcerate
debtors and bankrupts.
It contained some 300 prisoners and their families – often
forced to beg for money
from their cell windows.

812

Charles Dickens describes Fleet Prison
in his novel *Pickwick Papers*
and it also features in the *Rake's Progress*,
a series of eight pictures
by William Hogarth.
The prison was demolished in 1846.

Newgate Prison

This was built by Henry II in 1188 by
two carpenters and one smith at a cost of £3 6s 8d.

Newgate Prison was rebuilt in 1422, 1672
and 1780–88 – and demolished in 1902.

Prisoners at Newgate have included:

Daniel Defoe

William Kidd

Titus Oates

William Penn

Major Strangeways

816

Newgate appears in Dickens's *Barnaby Rudge*,
Oliver Twist and *Great Expectations*
and in William Thackeray's *Henry Esmond*.

817

Tyburn

Charles Dickens wrote of Tyburn:
'The gaol was a vile place in which most kinds of
debauchery and villainy were practised and where dire
diseases were bred that came into court with the prisoners,
and sometimes rushed straight from the dock at my Lord
Chief Justice himself and pulled him from the bench.
It had more than once happened that the Judge in the black
cap pronounced his own doom as certainly as the
prisoner's, and even died before him.'

1600s–1700s

Gaolers made money by selling spirits, candles, food
and water and releasing prisoners from irons.

Lice crunched underfoot in prisons and prisoners stank.
They had to be doused with vinegar
before being allowed into court.

1780

The Gordon Rioters broke Newgate Prison gates,
tore holes in the roof and set the prison alight.
Some 300 prisoners escaped in an hour
but many burned in the collapsing buildings.

1788

Punishments included hanging,
pressing, stocks, pillory, and whipping post.

pre-1890

Many criminals left Millbank Penitentiary
through a tunnel under the road
to enter barges on the Thames that took them to
transportation boats bound for Australia.
The Tate Gallery now occupies the site of the prison.

after 1868

Executions took place behind prison walls.

LONDON POLICE AND PRISONS

824

2001

In the UK, there were 60,000 people in prison care.

825

Clink Prison Museum has displays of prison life
and torture on the site of a small 16th-century prison.
Clink, the slang word for prison, derives from this prison.

826

The Black Museum of
New Scotland Yard is not open to the public.
This collection of criminal relics is
for police education and is the oldest museum
of its kind in the world.

The Black Museum has on display an awesome
variety of murder weapons as well as the death
masks of executed criminals.
They say that the hair still continues to grow
from one murderer's mask whose beard
was cut off before he was hanged.

A May Fayre and Puppet Festival in Covent Garden
includes Punch and Judy shows

EVENTS AND CEREMONY

For the Chinese New Year, processions and street entertainment include dragons and the famous Lion Dancers in Chinatown near Leicester Square.

the last Sunday in January

The anniversary of the execution of King Charles I is commemorated.
Hundreds of cavaliers march through central London in 17th-century dress, and prayers are said at the Banqueting House in Whitehall.

the last day before Lent

The Great Spitalfields Pancake Race celebrates Shrove Tuesday, when pancakes were made
to use up butter and eggs before the Lenten fast.
At Old Spitalfields Market, teams dress up to race, flipping pancakes.

831

1 March

On the closest Sunday to St David's Day,
a member of the Royal Family presents the Welsh Guards
with the principality's national emblem, a leek.

832

3 March

An Oranges and Lemons service is held at
St Clement Danes, the Strand, when,
as a reminder of the nursery rhyme,
children are presented with the fruits.
The church bells ring out the rhyme at
9am, noon, 3pm and 6pm.

833

5 April

The Harness Horse Parade is a celebation of heavy
working horses, wearing gleaming brass harnesses and
plumes, at Battersea Park.

834

early April

The University Boat Race takes place from Putney to
Mortlake as Oxford and Cambridge eights battle upstream.

835

April 21

The Queen's Official Birthday is celebrated with a 21-gun
salute in Hyde Park and by troops in parade dress
on Tower Hill at noon.

836

in April

In the London Marathon, some 30,000 competitors run from Greenwich Park to Buckingham Palace.

837

Through the summer in *Shakespeare Under the Stars*, the Bard's works are performed at the Open Air Theatre in Regent's Park.

838

the 2nd Sunday in May

A May Fayre and Puppet Festival in Covent Garden sees a procession, a service at St Paul's and Punch and Judy shows until 6pm at the site where Pepys watched England's first Punch and Judy show in 1662.

the 3rd Sunday in May

A Memorial Service is held for Pearly Kings and Queens
at St Martins-in-the-Fields.

in May

The Chelsea Flower Show, held in the grounds of Chelsea
Royal Hospital, exhibits the best of British gardening and is
attended by many celebrities.

841

in early June

The Retreat is beaten on drums by mounted regiments at a
colourful musical ceremony in Horse Guards Parade.

June to mid-August
The Royal Academy founded in 1768–
with Sir Joshua Reynolds as president
and Thomas Gainsborough as a member–
holds its Summer Exhibition of works
by living painters.

At the Royal Ascot Racecourse there are 24 race days
throughout the year, with the feature race meetings
being the Royal Meeting in June,
Diamond Day in late July,
and the Festival in late September.

June

Trooping the Colour at Horse Guards Parade in Whitehall
celebrates the official birthday of The Queen, who
inspects her regiments and takes their salute
as they parade before her.
The custom dates back to Charles II's reign when the
colours of a regiment were a rallying point in battle.
To ensure that every soldier could recognise the
colours of his own regiment at a glance,
they were trooped in front of the men every day.

Raising of the Thames Barrier: once a year a full test is done
on all 10 of the massive steel gates.

summer sporting events include:
Cricket's Second Test Match at
Lord's cricket ground, St John's Wood,
and the Lawn Tennis Championships held in Wimbledon
since 1877. The crowd at Wimbledon enjoy fine tennis –
and the traditional strawberries and cream.

July to mid-September
Promenade Concerts at the Royal Albert Hall attract
music enthusiasts from around the world.
These concerts were launched in 1895 and are the
principal summer venue for the
BBC Symphony Orchestra.

August

The Notting Hill Carnival is one of the largest street
festivals in Europe,
attracting more than a half-million people.
Live reggae and soul music combine
with great Caribbean food.

early autumn

The Horse of the Year Show is the premier
equestrian highlight on the English calendar.
Riders fly in from all continents.

October

The Costermongers' Pearly Harvest Festival at
St Martin-in-the-Fields, Trafalgar Square, is a harvest
thanksgiving attended by the Cockney Pearly
Kings and Queens.

1st Monday in October

The State Opening of Parliamen takes place at the House of
Lords when The Queen reads an official speech written by
the government of the day.
The monarch rides from Buckingham Palace to Westminster
in a royal coach accompanied by the Yeoman of the Guard
and the Household Cavalry.

1st Monday in October

At Westminster Abbey's Judges' Service, the judiciary mark
the opening of the law term. Then, in wigs and full regalia,
the judges process to the House of Lords for their
'Annual Breakfast'.

October's Quit Rents Ceremony

At the Royal Courts of Justice, an official receives token
rents on behalf of The Queen. The ceremony includes
splitting sticks and counting horseshoes.

November

The London-to-Brighton Veteran Run starts in Hyde Park.

5 November

Guy Fawkes' Night commemorates the Gunpowder Plot, an attempt to blow up King James I and his Parliament. Huge bonfires are lit throughout the city, and Guy Fawkes is burned in effigy.

about 11 November

Remembrance Sunday commemorates those members of the Services who died for their country in war.
The Queen, Prime Minister and other dignitaries lay wreaths and observe two minutes' silence at the Cenotaph.
Red poppies are worn as the symbol of this day.

2nd Saturday in November

The Lord Mayor's Procession goes from the Guildhall to the Royal Courts of Justice. Two miles of colourful floats mark the inauguration of the new Lord Mayor of London and his presentation to the monarch. The Queen must ask permission to enter the City's square mile – a right guarded by London merchants since the 1600s.

December

Carols are sung under the tall Norwegian Christmas tree in Trafalgar Square, presented in thanks to the British for their support during World War II.

31 December

Watch Night at St Paul's Cathedral is marked by a service at 11:30pm. Meanwhile thousands gather in Trafalgar Square to celebrate the New Year.

Every summer day and every other winter day

Detachments of the army's Household Division (consisting of seven regiments that have guarded the Royal Family since 1660) change the Guard outside Buckingham Palace. The New Guard marches to the Palace from Wellington Barracks and fresh sentries take up their positions as the Old Guard returns to barracks.

Every night at 10pm, the Ceremony of the Keys at the Tower of London sees the official handing over of the Tower keys, an event that has taken place for 700 years.

£25 for a lizard

£3,000 for a lion

£3,000 for a tiger

£6,000 for an elephant

FASCINATING TITBITS

In 1297 pigsties were banned from the streets of London

1861

Trams were introduced into London by a Mr Train.

The first public lavatory for ladies in London
was opened in 1884.
Up until then it had been considered that ladies
would be far too discreet to use a public facility.

In the Harry Potter films,
Little Whinging Zoo was filmed at London Zoo,
while Gringotts Bank is Australia House in the Strand.

865

Kings Cross Railway Station has become more popular
thanks to Harry Potter's 'Platform 9¾'
(actually filmed on Platform 4).

866

Although most pre-Roman 'Londoners'
only travelled up to 31 miles (50 km) in their lifetime,
some traded as far away as present-day Switzerland.

867

In prehistoric times,
lions, hippos, rhinos, straight-tusked elephants, deer, wild
horses, pigs and oxen
roamed the Thames Valley.

868

Many pieces in the current collection of Crown Jewels
were made for Charles II's coronation in 1661.
They are believed to be copies of the jewels lost
when the Commonwealth government took over
from the monarchy in 1649.

869

'Bouncer', the resident cat at the *Garrick Theatre*,
was once named as a shareholder.

870

The oldest royal coach still in use
is the Gold State Coach,
first used by George III
when he opened Parliament in 1821.

871

The most famous attempt to steal the Crown Jewels was made in 1671 by Colonel Thomas Blood, who was caught at the East Gate of the Tower of London with the crown and orb.

872

The Royal Family has a fleet of motor vehicles. Housed in the Royal Mews are 8 state limousines, 5 Rolls-Royces and 3 Daimlers. The Rolls-Royces have no number plates.

873

Brown's Hotel in Albermarle Street was where the first ever telephone call was made by Alexander Bell in 1876. Franklin and Eleanor Roosevelt spent their honeymoon here.

The first royal to travel in a motor car was Edward VII (before he was king). By 1902, he owned four Daimlers.

In 1875, young orphan Henry Croft worked in the markets and made friends with traders who collected money to help fellow 'costermongers' in need. They wore suits decorated with a row of pearl buttons. Henry adopted a 'Flash Boy Outfit' by covering it with tiny pearl buttons. At a local carnival, he raised funds for the orphanage – and was soon doing so for hospitals and churches.

Henry asked the costermongers to help and before long there was a Pearly Family for every London borough. When he died in 1930, Henry had collected over £5,000 (worth £200,000 today).

876

It seems Romans went swimming in the Thames:
an archaeological dig at Shadwell found
two Roman leather bikinis.

877

William Claridge bought existing hotel premises and
founded Claridge's Hotel,
after saving up his earnings as a butler.

878

Dogs supplied by Battersea Dogs Home helped the World
War II effort as sentries and Red Cross workers.
They were parachuted into minefields and
trained to lay wires across country under
concentrated fire and to carry ammunition.

The general public can 'adopt' many of the animals at
London Zoo. It costs:

£25 for a lizard

£35 for a jellyfish

£1,000 for a gorilla

£3,000 for a lion or tiger

£6,000 for an elephant

and £35 for a share in a larger animal.

Pêche Melba and Melba toast were first created at *The Savoy* in
the Strand, in honour of opera singer Dame Nellie Melba.

In 1297 pigsties were banned from the streets of London.

The Mousetrap by Agatha Christie
is the world's longest running play.
It had its 20,000th performance in December 2000
and was 50 years old in November 2002, by which time
some 10 million people had seen the play. An armchair and
clock are original props used in every performance.

In 1870, London music hall *The Alhambra* lost its licence
because its manager presented
'an indecent dance' called the can-can.

The last salmon fished from the Thames
was caught in June 1833.

The *Prospect of Whitby*, a riverside pub founded in 1520,
was frequented by Pepys, Dickens, Whistler and Turner.
Here in the 1700s a sailor sold an unknown plant collected
on his travels – the first fuchsia in England.

During World War II, the *Dorchester*
(later to be a favourite hotel of Elizabeth Taylor,
Peter Sellars and Charlton Heston)
was General Eisenhower's London HQ.

The Chelsea Physic Garden was established by
the Apothecaries' Company in 1676
to grow plants for research.

888

Harriet Westbrook, the deserted and pregnant first wife of the poet Percy Shelley, drowned herself in the Serpentine in December 1816.

889

Many hidden rivers still flow below the city. The Walbrook (between St Paul's and Mansion House) was covered over from 1463.

890

Changing names may confuse anyone studying the history of London Underground:
Aldwych was originally named Strand.
Embankment was originally Charing Cross.
Charing Cross was originally Strand.

891

The Fleet, once navigable as far as Holborn and wide enough to harbour pirates, was covered over from 1732.

892

Sir Christopher Wren's tiered spire of St Bride's, Fleet Street, inspired a local baker to create the first tiered wedding cake.

893

Londoners used to harvest excrement as a crop fertiliser, crawling on hands and knees to collect it, but the 'nightsoil men' lost their trade in 1847 when guano from South America began to be imported as a fertiliser.

Samuel Johnson

William Wordsworth

POEMS AND QUOTES

Joseph Addison 1672–1719

It was his considered opinion:

. . . that the Thames was the noblest river in Europe; that
London Bridge was a greater piece of work than any of the
Seven Wonders of the World; with many other honest
prejudices which naturally cleave to the
heart of a true Englishman.

Edmund C. Bentley 1875–1956

Sir Christopher Wren
Said, 'I am going to dine with some men.
If anyone calls
Say I am designing St Paul's.'

George Colman the Younger 1762–1836

Oh, London is a fine town,
A very famous city,
Where all the streets are paved with gold,
And all the maidens pretty.

Charles Dickens 1812–1870

Describing the Soho of the 1780s:

There were few buildings then, north of the Oxford-road,
and forest-trees flourished, and wild flowers grew, and the
hawthorn blossomed, in the now vanished fields. As a
consquence, country airs circulated in Soho with vigorous
freedom . . . and there was many a good south wall, not far
off, on which the peaches ripened in their season.

Charles Dickens 1812–1870

Describing the docks in the 1820s:

Down by the Docks, scraping fiddles go in the public houses all day long, and shrill, above . . . the din, rises the screeching of innumerable parrots brought from foreign parts.

Benjamin Disraeli 1804–1881

London: a nation, not a city.

Sir Arthur Conan Doyle 1859–1930

London, that great cesspool into which all the loungers of the Empire are irresistibly drained.

Gustave Doré 1832 – 83

The humours of the place are rough and coarse – as the perfomances in the penny gaffs and public-house sing-songs testify; but there is everywhere a readiness to laugh.

Sir Arthur Conan Doyle 1859–1930

His fictional detective Sherlock Holmes says:
It is my belief Watson, founded upon my experience, that the lowest and vilest alleys of London do not present a more dreadful record of sin than does the smiling and beautiful countryside.

Samuel Johnson 1709–84

Sir, if you wish to have a just notion of the magnitude of this city, you must not be satisfied with seeing its great streets and squares, but must survey the innumerable little lanes and courts. It is not in the showy evolutions of buildings, but in the multiplicity of human habitations which are crowded together, that the wonderful immensity of London consists.

Samuel Johnson 1709–84

Why, Sir, you find no man, at all intellectual, who is willing to leave London. No, Sir, when a man is tired of London, he is tired of life; for there is in London all that life can afford.

Samuel Johnson 1709–84

A country gentleman should bring his lady to visit London
as soon as he can, that they may have agreeable topicks for
conversation when they are by themselves.

906

Samuel Johnson 1709–84

The happiness of London is not to be conceived but by those
who have been in it.
I will venture to say, there is more learning and science
within the circumference of ten miles from where we now
sit, than in all the rest of the world.

Samuel Johnson 1709–84

By seeing London,

I have seen as much of life as the world can shew.

Edward Gibbon 1737–94

Crowds without company,

and dissipation without pleasure.

Hugo Meynell 1727–1808

The chief advantage of London is,

that a man is always so near his burrow.

A. A. Milne 1882–1956

They're changing guard at Buckingham Palace–

Christopher Robin went down with Alice.

Alice is marrying one of the guard.

'A soldier's life is terrible hard,'

Says Alice

William Morris 1834–96

Forget six counties overhung with smoke,

Forget the snorting steam and piston stroke,

Forget the spreading of the hideous town,

Think rather of the packhorse on the down,

And dream of London, small and white and clean,

The clear Thames bordered by its gardens green.

Alexander Pope 1688–1744

of the Monument to the Great Fire:

Where London's column, pointing at the skies,

Like a tall bully lifts the head, and lies.

Thomas De Quincey 1785–1859

It was a Sunday afternoon, wet and cheerless; and a duller
spectacle this earth of ours has not to show than a rainy
Sunday in London.

Percy Bysshe Shelley 1792–1822

Hell is a city much like London–
A populous and smoky city.

915

Ring-a-ring o' roses

Ring-a-ring o' roses
A pocket full of posies'
A–tishoo! A–tishoo!
We all fall down.

916

The origin of Ring-a-ring o' Roses is believed to be the Great
Plague of 1665. The roses refer to the rosy-coloured rash on
victims; the ring refers to the round 'tokens' which were
usually a sign of approaching death. The pocket was because
bags of herbs were carried to ward off plague and the
A–tishoo! was because sneezing was a symptom of the
disease.

Composed upon Westminster Bridge

Earth has not anything to show more fair:
Dull would he be of soul who could pass by
A sight so touching in its majesty:
This City now doth, like a garment, wear
The beauty of the morning; silent, bare,
Ships, towers, domes, theatres, and temples lie
Open unto the fields, and to the sky;
All bright and glittering in the smokeless air.
Never did sun more beautifully steep
In his first splendour, valley, rock, or hill;
Ne'er saw I, never felt, a calm so deep!
The river glideth at his own sweet will:
Dear God! the very houses seem asleep;
And all that mighty heart is lying still!

Composed upon Westminster Bridge was written by
William Wordsworth (1770 – 1850) on 3 September 1802.

Percy Bysshe Shelley 1792–1822

London, that great sea, whose ebb and flow
At once is deaf and loud, and on the shore
Vomits its wrecks, and still howls on for more.

H. G. Wells 1866–1946
1909

London . . . takes a lot of understanding. It's a great place. Immense.
The richest town in the world, the biggest port, the greatest
manufacturing town, the Imperial city – the centre of civilisation,
the heart of the world.

Oranges and Lemons

Oranges and lemons,

Say the bells of St Clement's.

You owe me five farthings,

Say the bells of St Martin's.

When will you pay me?

Say the bells at Old Bailey.

When I grow rich,

Say the bells at Shoreditch.

Pray, when will that be?

Say the bells at Stepney.

I'm sure I don't know,

Says the great bell at Bow.

Oranges and Lemons

This final verse does not appear in early versions:

Here comes a candle to light you to bed,

Here comes a chopper to chop off your head

Chop, chop, chop, chop, the last man's head!

Some claim it refers to Henry VIII's beheading of his wives.
Others say it was sung for Mary Queen of Scots as she went
to the scaffold. St Clement's church is most likely St
Clement Eastcheap – near the wharves where citrus fruits
were unloaded.

William Pitt

The parks are the lungs of London.

London Bridge is Falling Down

London Bridge is falling down,

Falling down, falling down,

London Bridge is falling down,

My fair lady.

The old London Bridge was burned in 1014, swept away by
a gale in 1091, burned again in 1136 and 1212–13.
In the severe winter of 1282, huge pieces of ice battered
away five arches, along with shops and houses. The bridge
was almost destroyed by fire again in 1633.

A new London Bridge was built in 1823 and another in 1967–72. The 1823 bridge was sold and transported to Arizona, to span the Little Thames River, a canal off the Colorado River.

COMMENTS BY LONDON
UNDERGROUND DRIVERS

926

Heard on the Piccadilly Line:
This is Knightsbridge Station. All change here for Mr Fayed's little corner shop.

927

At Camden Town station on a crowded Saturday afternoon:
Please let the passengers off the train first . . .
Please let the passengers off the train first . . .
Please let the passengers off the train first . . .
Let the passengers off the train FIRST! . . .
Oh go on then, stuff yourselves in like sardines, see if I care,
I'm going home!

928

On the Central Line:
Ladies and Gentlemen, I do apologise for the delay to your
service. I know you're all dying to get home, unless, of
course, you happen to be married to my ex-wife, in which
case you'll want to cross over to the Westbound and go in
the opposite direction.

929

At West Hampstead:

We can't move off because some c*** has their f***ing hand
stuck in the door.

930

At Mill Hill East:

Hello this is . . . speaking. I am the captain of your train,
and we will be departing shortly. We will be cruising at an
altitude of approximately zero feet, and our scheduled
arrival time in Morden is 3.15pm. The temperature in
Morden is approximately 15 degrees celsius, and Morden is
in the same time zone as Mill Hill East, so there's no need
to adjust your watches.

RIVER THAMES

931

The Thames took its present course *c.* 450,000 years ago.

932

The first bridge across the Thames was a wooden construction, built by the Romans in AD 50.

933

Old London Bridge was one of the wonders of the medieval world. Built between 1176–1209, the stone bridge was the longest in Europe at that time.

934

Swans were first brought to London during Richard I's reign. The Thames swans belong to the Dyers' company, the Vintners or the monarch.

935

The Marine Police Force, founded to protect ships in 1798,
is the oldest police force in the world.

936

Moored at Greenwich, the *Cutty Sark* (built 1869) was the
fastest tea-clipper in the world,
sailing from London to China in 107 days.

937

There were great Thames floods in 1236, 1663, 1894,
1915, 1928, 1929, 1947, 1953 and 1963.
Since 1965 the Thames Barrier has prevented floods.

938

In 1895, ice smashed barges in the Pool of London.

939

In 1564–5 there was archery, dancing and an ox roast on the frozen Thames, with booths from Temple to Southwark.

940

There were Frost Fairs on the Thames in 1683, 1698 1740 and 1814.
At 1814's Frost Fair, fires were lit and sheep roasted.
On 5 February, the thaw sent fires hissing
into the water, and some people drowned.

941

Cromwell's coach and horses sank on the Lambeth ferry.

942

The arches of the old London Bridge slowed water flow and made it easier for oarsmen to row against the tide.

943

Once the old London Bridge was demolished in 1831, the Thames no longer froze.

944

At the end of the 1500s some 40,000 people were employed on the river,

945

Merchants left bequests to 'God and the Bridge', and the Bridge House Estates Fund grew with interest. It is now worth an annual income of over £12 million.

946

In 1633, the Lambeth ferry sank under the weight of an archbishop's belongings.

947

When Westminster Bridge was built, the Thames watermen were paid £25,000 in compensation.

948

Italian banker Roberto Calvi was found hanging underneath Blackfriars Bridge on 18 June 1982.

949

In 1536 a baby girl fell from London Bridge into the river but was rescued by an apprentice – whom she eventually married and who became Lord Mayor of London.

From shore to shore the old London Bridge was nearly 350 yards (318 metres) long on 19 piers.

At the Southwark end of London Bridge, the severed heads of traitors, parboiled and tarred, were displayed on spikes.

Tower Bridge opens fully within 90 seconds to allow the passage of large ships.

Opened in 1894, Tower Bridge had steam engines which raised the 1,000-ton bascules.
In 1976 the system was electrified.

In 1951, a number 78 bus found itself stranded when the bridge began to open. The driver accelerated and cleared the gap safely. He was rewarded with a medal and £10 from public funds.

RIVER PUBS

A Georgian riverside pub, *The Anchor*, is where Dr Johnson wrote parts of his dictionary and Dickens drank. It is now famous as the pub where Tom Cruise enjoys a pint at the end of the film *Mission Impossible*.

At Hammersmith, the 17th-century *Dove* boasts the world's smallest public bar. Here *Rule Britannia* was composed and Nell Gwynne and Charles II met to drink.

Julius Caesar named the river Tamesis,
the second oldest place-name in England, after Kent.

The London Apprentice was popular with artists Zoffany,
Constable and Turner.

Convicts awaiting transportation to Australia used to be
chained in the the *Town of Ramsgate* cellars.

960

The *Prospect of Whitby* is one of the oldest river pubs,
first built 1520.
Its name changed from *The Devil Tavern* when
the *Prospectic*, a colliery ship from Whitby,
moored nearby.

961

The London Apprentice at Isleworth looks out on to
Isleworth Ait island. This nature reserve is home to bats,
herons and the rare two-lipped door snail.

962

At the *Town of Ramsgate*, infamous Judge Jeffreys was
caught in 1688 and taken to the Tower of London.

The *Town of Ramsgate* used to be known as *The Red Cow*,
some say after its red-haired barmaid.

The *Black Lion*, Hammersmith,
is a 1700s haunted pub.
As the *Black Swan* it featured in A. P. Herbert's
The Water Gypsies.

Tattershall Castle on the Victoria Embankment
is a pub that was an old paddle steamer.

Short of money after the Crusades,
Richard I granted the City Corporation fishing rights
and control of the Thames
in 1197 for 1,500 marks.

1857

The Crown claimed ownership in an argument
that lasted 17 years
until the City gave way and the
Thames Conservancy Act was passed.

Thames Head, the source of the river,
is a small spring in Gloucestershire.

969

The River Thames is 210 miles (338 km)
from its source to the North Sea.

970

The Romans first embanked the Thames.
In 1868–74 Sir Joseph Bazalgette's great scheme reclaimed
32 acres of mud,
building 3½ miles (5.63 km) of banks
to prevent flooding and enclose sewers.

971

Mudlarks were children who scoured the river
mud at low tide, collecting anything that could be sold.
Toshers did the same in the sewer network.

In its heyday, the Port of London handled up to 52 million tonnes of cargo a year

FACTS AND FIGURES

Westminster Abbey, one of London's major historic attractions, is visited by 49 million people every year.

London has over 12,000 restaurants and cafés plus some 5,250 pubs and bars employing over 130,000 people.

Over 300,000 people work in the City of London but most of these commute – only about 4,500 people actually live there.

12.5% of the UK population live in London.

The City of London (from Temple Bar in the west to the Tower of London in the east) occupies an area of little more than one square mile (2.59 sq km).

976

London lies some 50 miles from the mouth of the Thames, latitude 51°30', longitude 0°5'.

977

Greater London is the largest metropolis in Western Europe, with an area of 625 sq miles (1620 sq km) and a population of 6–7 million residents.

978

47% of London's population are aged 16 to 44.
25% of London's population are over 65.

979

About 16.7% of Britain's workforce have jobs in London.
25% of all unemployed people in Britain live in London.

Nearly 700,000 people, almost 20% of London's workforce, work in cultural and creative sectors.

Over 250 languages are spoken in London.

London has 33 boroughs, including the City of London.

Lambeth has the highest population of an inner London borough with 267,000 residents.

London has over 150 historic buildings and ancient monuments.

985

Croydon is the highest populated outer London borough, with 332,000 residents.

986

The most densely populated borough is Kensington & Chelsea with 13,120 residents per sq km.

987

Over 25% of the world's largest companies have their European HQs in London.

988

Almost 33% of London is green space or parks – more than any other city of its size in the world.

London has three world-heritage sites (Tower of London,
Maritime Greenwich and Westminster Abbey).

Within London are:
3 country parks
5 symphony orchestras
33 historic gardens
200 museums
500 cinema screens.

The Port of London covers about 150 km (93 miles) of
waterway along the Thames to the east coast and handles
some 52 million tonnes of cargo a year (1995).

Within an hour of London are:

2 county cricket clubs

6 racecourses

7 ice rinks

12 professional football teams

37 rowing clubs

50 athletics tracks

95 golf courses

546 swimming pools

2,000 tennis courts.

Average January temp: 43°F (6°C)

Average July temp: 66°F (19°C)

Annual rainfall: 32 inches (799mm)

London has 20,000 licensed taxis.

In 2002, 28 million people visited London for at least one night, spending £8.6 billion.

49 million people visit London's attractions every year. Nearly 50% of these are from overseas.

The 12 inner boroughs that surround the City are Westminster, Camden, Islington, Hackney, Tower Hamlets, Greenwich, Lewisham, Southwark, Lambeth, Wandsworth, Hammersmith and Fulham, Kensington and Chelsea.

The 20 outer boroughs are Waltham Forest, Redbridge, Havering, Barking and Dagenham, Newham, Bexley, Bromley, Croydon, Sutton, Merton, Kingston-upon-Thames, Richmond-upon-Thames, Hounslow, Hillingdon, Ealing, Brent, Harrow, Barnet, Haringe, and Enfield.

The Thames Path is the longest riverside walk in Europe.

Richmond Bridge is the oldest surviving Thames bridge (built 1774).

The University of London is the largest in the UK.

London's universities include:

Birkbeck of London

Thames Valley University

University College London

Queen Mary, University of London

King's College London

Institute of Education

London Guildhall University

South Bank University

The London Institute

University of Greenwich

University of North London

University of Westminster

General disclaimer

While the compiler and publishers of this volume have acted in good faith as collators of information they can in no way be held responsible or accept liability for any loss or damage arising, howsoever caused.